THE UNORTHODOX BOOK OF JEWISH RECORDS & LISTS

Allan Gould & Danny Siegel

SAMUEL WACHTMAN'S SONS

Wachtman's Sons

An Imprint of the Millennium Publishing Group

Library of Congress Cataloging-in-Publication Data
        Gould, Allan
        Siegel, Danny
        The Unorthodox Book of Jewish Records and Lists
        Illustrations by David Shaw
        192 p. cm
        CIP No.
        ISBN 1-88882-004-7
        1. Jews - Anecdotes
        2. Jewish humor
        3. Humor

Cover Design by David Shaw
Author photograph by Stephen Epstein

Printed in the United States of America

2 4 6 8 9 7 5 3 1

The Longest Table of Contents
in a Book of Jewish Records and Lists

Dedication/9
A Note on the Research Methods Used in Compiling This Book/10

I   Words, Words, Words
(and an Occasional Phrase Thrown In, Free)

The Most Impressive Answers to the Statement,
    "You don't look Jewish"/13
The Most Common Jewish Expressions/14
Little-known Jewish Greetings/14
The Greatest Lyrics of Hassidic Tunes/16
The Most Boring Lecture Given at an American
    Jewish Community Center/17
Famous Clichés and Their Jewish Origins/18

II   Books, Scrolls, Papyrus and Cave Scribblings

Shakespeare's Jewish Inspiration/21
Jewish Authors Who Have Not Been Considered for
    the Nobel Prize for Literature/23
The Smallest Manuscript of the Five Books of Moses/24
The Shortest Jewish Book/24
The Funniest Works of Fiction Ever Written by Jews/26

III   Israel—Home Free

Great Inventions Which Have Come Out of the Jewish State/29
The Most Unusual Stamps Issued by the State of Israel/30
The Best Excuses for Not Making Aliyah/31
The Most Incompetent Israeli Tour Guide/31
Famous Non-Meetings of Famous Jews/33
The Most Common Answers Given by Israelis to the Question,
    "How long are you here for, in North America?"/34

IV   Philanthropy
(and the High Cost of Giving)

The Most Persistent United Jewish Appeal Solicitors/37
Little-known Jewish Charities/38
Discredited Jewish Fund-raising Techniques/38
The Most Donor Plaques per Square Foot/40

V Jewish History
(Ancient, Modern and Sometimes Even Tolerable)

The Earliest Jewish Traffic Signs/43
The Oldest Jewish Notes/44
The Most Courageous Speeches Given by Jews/44
Famous Last Words of Jewish Heroes/45
The Seven Wonders of the Ancient Jewish World/47
The Worst Jewish Famines/48
Great Jewish Battles/48
The Lost Tribes of Israel/49
The Most Dangerous Jewish Occupations in History/50
The Most Important Groups Founded by Jews/52
Jewish Coats of Arms/52
The Original, Jewish Names of the Seven Dwarfs/53
The Earliest Known Jewish Musical Groups/54
Jews Who Have Bought Things Retail/56
The Longest Undiscovered Marrano/57
Actions Which Can Predict the Coming of the Messiah/58

VI Synagogues, Rabbis, Cantors
(and other Mixed Blessings)

The Shortest Jewish Sermons/61
The Longest Sermons Delivered in a Synagogue/62
The Strangest Titles of Jewish Sermons/63
The Worst Faux Pas Made at a Jewish Funeral/63
The Shortest Tenure of a Jewish Rabbi/64
The Shortest Tenure of a Cantor/65
The Largest Synagogue in the World/66
The Smallest Synagogue/67
The Worst Names of Synagogues/68
The Highest Bima/68
The Most Common Lines from Bar Mitzvah Speeches/69
The Highest Temperature in a Synagogue Where a
    Woman Wore a Mink Stole/71
The Most Expensive High Holiday Tickets Not Used/71
The Best Tunes for "Adon Olam"/72
The Most Successful "Alternative Minyans"/72
The Most Miserly Kiddish Given by a Jew/73
The Least Self-conscious Man at a Sabbath Kiddish/73

VII   Jewish Rituals
(and Other Things to Rebel Against)

The Sloppiest Bris in History/77
The Fastest Ritual Circumcision of a Jewish Child/78
Songs Traditionally Sung at Ritual Circumcisions/78
The Hardest Jewish Puzzle in History/79
The Most Commonly Used Texts for "Creative" Jewish Weddings/80
The Most Popular Songs Played at Jewish Weddings/81
The Classiest Conclusion of a Jewish Wedding Ceremony/82
The Most Vulgar Jewish Funerals/83
The Shortest Shiva/84
The Dietary Laws/84
Mitzvot Which All Jews Follow/85
Little-known Jewish Blessings/86
The Fastest Shacharit/87
The Yarmulka and Its Derivatives/88
The Most Expensive Yarmulkas/89
The Weirdest Materials for a Skullcap/89
The Most Words and Weirdest Inscriptions on a Yarmulka/90
The Longest Payos Worn by a Religious Jew/90
The Curliest Sidelocks/92
The Most Ostentatious Mezuzah/92
The Sexiest Shaytel/93
The Least-used Bar Mitzvah Gifts/94

VIII   The Jewish Calendar
(and Other Timely Concerns)

Little-known Jewish Holy Days/97
The Best Way to Remember the Jewish Calendar/98
The Worst Things a Jew Can Eat Before the Yom Kippur Fast/99
The Most People in a Sukkah/100
The Classiest Sukkah/100
The Shortest Time to Kosher a Stove for Passover/101
The Largest Etrog/103
The Most Generous Afikoman Gift Ever Recorded/104

IX   The Jewish Family
(Plus Related Joys and Horrors)

The Most Popular Jewish Names for Children in the 1960s, 1970s
    and 1980s/107
The Jewish Life Cycle/108
The Most Successful Son to Go into His Father's Business/108

The Most Common Names of Jewish Girls in
    Haight-Ashbury in the 1960s/109
The Most Popular Jewish Name Changes/110
The Most Popular Names for Jewish Girls in the
    Southern United States/111
The Most Macho Names Given to Jewish Male Children/111
The Most Popular Heroes of Jewish Kids/112
The Smartest Jewish Grandchild/113
The Most "Kvelling" Jewish Grandparents/113
The Rottenest Child of the Nicest Jewish Parent/114
The Greatest One-liner Guilt Trips Laid upon a Jewish
    Child by a Jewish Mother/115
The Most Spiteful Jewish Daughter-in-law/116
The Jewish Child Who Stayed Home the Longest/116
The Most Rebellious Jewish Child/117
The Most Sexist Jewish Birth Announcements/118
The Longest Time a Bubbe Not Visited/119
People with Whom Jews May Not Have Sexual Relations/120

X Food
(Nourishment, Noshes, Nibbles, Fressing and Other Jewish Obsessions)

Classic Jewish Foods and Their Christian Counterparts/123
Kosher Wines, According to Sweetness/124
The Most Jews Ever Seen in a Chinese Restaurant/125
The Most Chinese Ever Seen in a Jewish Restaurant/125
The Earliest Known Jewish Graces after Meals/126
The Most Elaborate Bar/Bat Mitzvah Foods/127
The Longest Period of Time Any Jew Has Waited for a
    Corned Beef Sandwich/129
The Largest Challah Ever Baked/130
The Largest Challah Ever Burnt to a Crisp/131
Great Jewish Diets/131
The Largest Matzah Ball in History/132
The Sharpest Horseradish Ever Served with Gefilte Fish/135
The Driest Jewish Boiled Chicken Recipe/135
The Largest Piece of Matzah/136
The Greasiest Latke/137
The Saltiest Lox/138
The Most Versatile Jewish Food/139
The Most Carp in a Single Jewish Bathtub/141
The Most Ecumenical Jewish Dishes/142

XI Jews in Suburbia
(and Other Chosen Ghettos)

The Most Exclusive Jewish Country Club/145
The Most Needless Examples of Wall-to-Wall Carpeting/146
The Best Greetings to Jewish Nose-job Patients/147
The Most Luxurious Kosher Vacation Hideaway/148
Jewish Cases of Spontaneous Combustion/148
Strange Customs of Rare Jewish Communities and Sects/151
The Most Commonly Given Excuses for a Jewish Child
    to Miss Hebrew School/152
The Synagogues That Held Out the Longest Before
    Being Forced to Move/152
The Biggest Show-offs in Jewish Suburbia/153

XII Occupations
(Doctors of the Mind and Body Plus Some Jews Who Couldn't Stand the Sight of Blood)

The Most Common Jewish Occupations
    of the Twentieth Century/157
Typical Salaries for Employees in Jewish Communal Work
    in Major North American Cities, 1989/158
The Jewish Stress Scale/158
Famous Jewish Law Firms/159
Famous Jewish Marksmen/161
Specifically Jewish Diseases/161
Famous Jewish Mountain Climbers/162
The Most Jewish Doctors/164
The Fewest Jewish Doctors/165
The Most Overwhelming Act of Bikur Cholim/165
The Schmaltziest Jewish Violinist/166

XIII Inventors
(Breakthroughs and Breakdowns)

Jews Who Never "Made It"/169
Inventions Jews Will Invent Before Long/170
Great Jewish Conversions/171
The Fastest Jew on Land/173
Famous Mistakes in the World of Science/173
A List of Ancient Jewish Measurements
    and Their Recent Usage/174

XIV Jewish Records and Lists Which Didn't Fit Into Any Topic for Reasons Too Numerous to List
(or we'd have to include another list)

The Most Countries One Jew Had to Leave/177
People Who Should Have Been Jewish, and Probably Are
   If They Go Back Far Enough/178
The Oldest Known Jewish Nursery Rhyme/178
The Toughest Hassidim/179
Little-known Jewish Superstitions/181
Jews Will Rogers Never Met Or He Never Would Have
   Said: "I never met a man I didn't like"/181
The Longest Period of Time Any Jew Ever Spoke Without
   Using His Hands to Gesture/182
The Most Famous Scores in Religious Texts/184
The Longest-living Jews on Record/185
Jewish Origins of Famous Places/186

Glossary/187

Dedication

Most books have dedication pages, so how can this one set a new Jewish record? How about by name-dropping:

Thank you for some wonderful ideas. Al and Ruby Newman (he's a gastroenterologist, she's a wonderful teacher); Lisa Newman (she's a superb social worker, and no relation to Al and Ruby); Bobby and Sharon Silberstein (he's a flourishing businessman, she's a successful lawyer, and they've got beautiful twin sons); Professor Arnold Ages and his wife, Dr. Shoshana (he teaches French literature in one university, she teaches Hebrew at another); Rabbi Martin and Ruth Lockshin (he's not only a rabbi, but a teacher of Jewish Studies at a secular university, and she's a LaLeche Leader); David Shaw, our masterful artist; and Matie Molinaro, our literary agent, who bled Stoddart dry until she got the kind of contract she thought we deserved. And our parents, who always laugh, whether we are trying to be funny or not. And most of all, thanks to Merle Gould, wife of one of the two the authors of this *narishkeit*, and a magnificent English teacher in her own right. But *little* thanks to Judah and Elisheva Gould, who drive their father crazy, but then he remembers what a rotten kid *he* was at their ages, so there's still hope.

Now, does this dedication page set a record for *shepping nachas* or not?

And one more: for Abe and Shulamit Gittelson, in whose house DS wrote his first book, a volume of soaring lyrical poetry. We've come a long way, Abe and Shu.

A Note on the Research Methods Used in Compiling This Book

It takes more than two warped minds to put together a book such as this. Any Ph.D. candidate would be proud of the methods used: hundreds of interviews with Jews from the Malagasy Republic to Taiwan to Pittsburgh; telephone calls that have set a new record ("The Highest Private Phone Bill by a Pair of Jews Working on a Book of Jewish Records and Lists"); long, arduous hours spent in the great Jewish and secular libraries of the world (The Jewish Theological Seminary, Hebrew University, YIVO, Harvard University, and the Bathurst Heights Library, five blocks from one of our houses); and consultations with the leading scholars in such diverse fields as Yiddish Culture, Hebrew Grammar, Archaeology, Talmud, Medieval Jewish History, Ethnomusicology, and Orthodontia, as if they all had nothing better to do.

Hundreds upon hundreds of records and lists came to our attention: "The Most Tuna Fish Sandwiches Eaten by a Kosher-eating Jew on a Road Trip"; "Slowest Hebrew Typist"; "Longest Surviving Close Jewish Friend of Joseph Stalin"— these are just some of the lists that ended up on the cutting room floor as we were forced to reduce the selection to a bare minimum in accordance with the ancient Jewish doctrine against causing unnecessary suffering to other human beings.

We have tried to be honest and accurate, often to no avail. Some of the manuscripts examined were blurred with age or spilt coffee, so dates may be off by a year or two. Some of the interviewees were blurred with age as well, so some spelling and names might also be off. Don't be so picky. Look, we have tried our best. And that's a lot more than a lot of political leaders have done, you've got to admit.

Allan Gould Danny Siegel
Toronto, Ont. Rockville, Md.
January 1997 January 1997

10

I
Words, Words, Words
(and an Occasional Phrase
Thrown In, Free)

The Most Impressive Answers to the Statement, "You don't look Jewish"

Since time immemorial, which is pretty long, Jews have been approached by non-Jews and told, "Gee, you don't *look* Jewish." Whether the remark is intended as a compliment, suggesting that the said person is lucky to lack the dreadful features of the "average" Jew, or merely as a harmless comment about hair colouring and physical condition (green? three eyes?), it continues to be stated to thousands of Jews every single day of every year.

1   "Funny, *you* don't look anti-Semitic."
2   "Thanks. Neither do you."
3   "*Really*? Well, that helps explain why they let me join your country club last week."
4   "Oh? That's only because I left my beard at home."
5   "If you saw me in the shower, you wouldn't say that." (For men only)
6   "I know, I know. That's why I finally converted to Unitarianism."
7   "At many points in our history, that has been a distinct advantage."

The Most Common Jewish Expressions

Every cultural, national, and religious group has its own expressions which are peculiar to it. The British say "old chap." The Canadians affix "eh?" to the end of almost every sentence. The Russians always add the curious phrase "How much you want for your jeans?" to all greetings to foreigners. Indeed, one could go on and on, inviting the resentment of a hundred different groups.

And the Jews' most common expressions? Read on.

1   "Oy vey iz mir."
2   "Mazel tov."
3   "What time is the next boat to America?"
4   "Leave me alone, or I'll call the police."
5   "What do you mean, you *are* the police?"
6   "Gevalt!"
7   "Happy holiday!"
8   "Are you single? I've got a wonderful daughter/son."
9   "Abi gezunt."
10   "Yes, you can have my coat and all my luggage. Just let me get on that boat to America."

Little-known Jewish Greetings

There are some standard, automatic greetings that everyone knows about. For example, when a Jewish mother meets a Jewish doctor (male or female) between the ages of 25 and 38, her greeting is: "Are you married?" But there are many Jews out there who are not doctors (or if they are then they are over or under age, or obviously married); even so, these people must be greeted.

1   "Hot enough for ya?" is a greeting almost exclusive to the Jews of Southern Florida, especially along the east coast.

2 "Cold enough for ya?" was the invariable greeting of the Jews of northern Russia, including Siberia. This remnant of their cultural tradition lives on among many of their descendants who brought it with them to Montreal, and particularly to Winnipeg.

3 "Violent enough for ya?" was a greeting which became quite common among Jews of Eastern Europe in the nineteenth and early twentieth centuries.

4 "Hey, wanna buy a ticket for the boat to America?" was the salutation of the most popular Jews in nineteenth and twentieth century Europe.

The Greatest Lyrics of Hassidic Tunes

The Hassidim became a major part of modern Judaism in the eighteenth and nineteenth centuries. Most people know little about these deeply religious, passionate members of the Jewish world beyond *Fiddler on the Roof*, some short stories of I. B. Singer, and their music—joyous, exciting melodies and words celebrating God, life, and the world.

It is with great pleasure that this book presents, for the first time in print, some of the best-loved lyrics of Hassidic songs.

YA BA BA BA, YA BA BA BA, YA BA BA BA BA BA BA BA BA BAAAAAA,
YA BA BA BA, YA BA BA BA, YA BA BA BA BA BA BA BA BA BAAAAAA.
(The above is repeated two dozen times, interspersed with the
following chorus.)
Chorus: YA BABABABABABABABABABABABABABA, YA
BABABABABABABABABA
YA BABABABABABABABABABABABABABA, YA
BABABABABABABABABA

LAI DE DIE, LAI DE DIE, LAI DE DIE DIE DIE DIE DIE DIE DIE DIEEEEE.
LAI DE DIE, LAI DE DIE, LAI DE DIE DIE DIE DIE DIE DIE DIE DIEEEEE.
(These verses are repeated until the arrival of the Messiah, or
the onset of exhaustion, whichever comes first.)

OY BOY OY BOY OY BOY BOY BOY BOY BOY BOYYYYYYY
OY BOY OY BOY OY BOY BOY BOY BOY BOY BOYYYYYYY!! (HEY!!)

BIM, BAM, BIM BAM, BIM BAM, BIMBAMBIMBAMBIMBAMBIMBAMBIM-
BAMMMMMMM!
(Repeat, sing again, echo, and continue until dawn.)

LA LA LA LA LA LA LA LA LA — OYOYOYOYOYOYOYYYYYOOOOOOY!
LA LA LA LA LA LA LA LA LA — OYOYOYOYOYOYOYYYYYOOOOOOY!!
(repeated 613 times, followed by the chorus, sung endlessly)
Chorus: HEY HEY HEY HEY, OYOYOYOYOOOOOOOOOY!
HEY HEY HEY HEY, OYOYOYOYOOOOOOOOOY!

The Most Boring Lecture Given at an American Jewish Community Center

---

Jews have often been called the People of the Book. Whether
this refers to the Bible or to Irving Wallace and Sidney Sheldon
is still not clear. There is little question that Jews have tended
to read books over the past four millennia; sometimes they
even buy them, thank God. But Jews have not restricted their
search for knowledge to the written word alone. Over the centuries, they have also sought to learn orally from scholars. Lec-
tures from a great rabbi could be wonderful. But at other
times . . .

"Vowel Structures in Thirteenth Century Epic Hebrew Poetry in North African Centres of Jewish Population" were expounded upon by Ludwig Amadeus Freedman of Brandeis University, at Ann Arbor, Michigan, April 22–23, 1974.

Dr. Freedman was paid $600, plus expenses to and from Massachusetts. He had been "highly recommended" by Greta Lewin, the head of the Sisterhood of B'nai Banim in Ann Arbor, who was later discovered to be the lecturer's youngest sister. Even Mrs. Lewin, who loves her brother very much, found herself urgently needed at home after the first twenty minutes.

Famous Clichés and Their Jewish Origins

Not only have Jews engendered major religions, such as Christianity and Islam (we've given up waiting for a thank you), but they have also been the originators of many phrases that later became popular figures of speech, even clichés. While you probably will recognize most of the lines below, you are about to learn, for the first time, how many come from Jewish roots.

1 "I came, I saw, I was conquered." (Rabbi Aaron the Coward, Jerusalem, 70 of the Common Era)

2 "It's unbelievable! I can't believe my *eye!*" (Moshe Dayan, Sharm-el-Sheikh, 1967)

3 "I will have this signed, sealed, and maybe delivered." (Lou Shumsky, postman, the Bronx, 1935)

4 "There is no bomb in Gilead." (Explosives expert Yossi Yechiel Oz, Israel, November 28, 1973)

5 "I make profits without honour in my own country." (Harvey Rothschild, Paris, 1900)

6 "As ye sue, so shall I reap." (Noah Cohen, famous Los Angeles divorce lawyer, 1958)

II
Books, Scrolls,
Papyrus and
Cave Scribblings

Shakespeare's Jewish Inspiration

Over the centuries, many scholars have attempted to trace the origins of Shakespeare's plots: plays of Marlowe and Kyd, Holinshed's *Chronicles*, actual history. But until the publication of this book, no one has ever been aware of the extent to which Shakespeare actually owed *lines of dialogue* to a Jew, Chaim Blotnik. Probably the least known but most talented British playwright who lived before Shakespeare, Blotnik wrote many plays between 1540 and 1580, primarily on Jewish themes (which may explain why they weren't box office successes in the relatively Jew-free world of Elizabethan England).

Uncovered only recently in a Salvation Army bookstore in Toronto by one of the writers of this book, the plays of Blotnik, "the Beard of Avon," are shocking in their obvious influence upon the writing of the much better known Shakespeare. Whether the neglect of Blotnik is due to anti-Semitism, or mere oversight, we shall leave to the reader's imagination.

BLOTNIK

Sure I'm a Yid. But I can see, can't I? And don't I got a keppel, pulkas, feelings? I mean, really!
The Salesman of Manchester
(V, ii, 452)

SHAKESPEARE

I am a Jew! Hath not a Jew eyes? Hath not a Jew hands, organs, dimensions, senses, affections, passions?
The Merchant of Venice
(III, i, 62)

BLOTNIK	SHAKESPEARE

Boy, is it cold! Such a wind!
But what's colder than a kid
Who never drops his dad a
line?
Not much, lemme tell you.
Try It You'll Like It
(I, iv, 27)

Blow, blow, thou winter wind!
Thou art not so unkind
As man's ingratitude.
As You Like It
(II, vii, 174)

Rebono Shel Olam, these
guys are dummies!
Such a Dream I Had!
(II, iv, 7)

Lord, what fools these mor-
tals be!
A Midsummer Night's Dream
(III, ii, 115)

Ach, that music, it sounds
good enough to eat. Keep
playing, I'm hungry.
Hanukkah Lasts Eight Days
(V, iii, 18)

If music be the food of love,
play on.
Twelfth Night
(I, i, 1)

Be careful! Turn the evil eye;
Tu B'Shvat might be
unlucky!
When in Rome
(III, iv, 291)

Beware the Ides of March.
Julius Caesar
(I, ii, 18)

Such a rotten kid! She's like a
snake, is what she is. She
should only have kids that
treat her like she has treated
me!
*The Rotten Kids Who Caused
Their Father Heartache*
(I, ii, 77)

How sharper than a serpent's
tooth it is
To have a thankless child!
King Lear
(I, iv, 312)

So let's *do* it, already!
Let's get it over with!
So come on! Nu?
The Unethical King-Killers
(III, ii, 17)

If it were done when 'tis
done, then 'twere well
It were done quickly.
Macbeth
(I, vii, 1)

BLOTNIK	SHAKESPEARE
For *mishpacha*, he's not such a nice guy. You know? *The Nasty King-Killer* (II, iv, 12)	A little more than kin, and less than kind. *Hamlet* (I, ii, 65)
You should rot in hell, if anyone so much as lays a hand on my grave. Even in death, I can't get no respect. Blotnik's Epitaph	Cursed be he that moves my bones. Shakespeare's Epitaph

---

Jewish Authors Who Have Not Been Considered for the Nobel Prize for Literature

---

Isaac Bashevis Singer. Saul Bellow. John Steinberg. Ernest Hemingwasser. It's incredible, isn't it? The Jews, so small in number, have loomed so large among Nobel Laureates for Literature. But, hard as it is for the Jews to accept, not every Jew who has put quill to paper or fingers to typewriter has been considered by Sweden for the Ultimate Prize. Here are some we've dug up, so far:

Fanny Griesdorf of Madison, Wisconsin, who wrote a series of romantic novels for Vanity Press International, including *Nurse and Doctor* and its bestselling sequels— *Doctor and Nurse; The Nursing Doctor; Patient, Nurse, and Doctor; The Patient Nurse; The Doctored Nurse;* and *The Doctor's Patients.*

Jack Goldstein, author of *Gagged, Bound, and Whipped,* as well as *Sexy Susan Sins with Stevie* and *The Perverted Pathologist,* for He-Man Press, New York.

Allan Gould and Danny Siegel for *The Unorthodox Book of Jewish Records and Lists.* Damn it. (See back cover of this book.)

The Smallest Manuscript of the Five Books of Moses

The Torah, alias the Pentateuch, a.k.a. Five Books of Moses, is usually hand-written by scribes on large sheets of parchment, according to a set of very stringent rules. However, in response to a contest held in Jerusalem, Israel, in 1973, the following entries were submitted:

The entire Five Books of Moses was inscribed inside a Coca Cola bottlecap by Rabbi Moshe Schiffman of B'nai Brak, Israel. "Now *that's* the real thing!" he said, polishing his thick horn-rimmed glasses.

Rabbi Yitzchak ben Canaan of Crown Heights, Brooklyn, inscribed the Torah on a fountain pen which, he explained, he had received for his Bar Mitzvah over thirty years previously. "I could never find a use for it before now," the Rabbi stated later.

The entire Five Books of Moses, plus the Books of Joshua and Kings I, were inscribed on the head of a pin by Rabbi Dr. Sol H. Tanenbaum of St. Paul, Minnesota. The prize-winning scientist/scholar absent-mindedly patted his new seeing-eye dog, Ora, as he described his revolutionary laser gun technique.

The Shortest Jewish Book

From *Interpretation of Dreams* (Freud) to *Henderson the Rain King* (Bellow) to *The Brothers Karamazov* (Dostoyevsky—you didn't *know*?), great Jewish books have tended to be rather lengthy. Not so with the following record-holder:

Names, Addresses, and Occupations of the Jews of Spain, published by Moshe Cardozo de Pinta in 1492, was to have

been over 2,500 pages long. But with the expulsion of the entire Jewish community in October of that year, Mr. Cardozo de Pinta immediately had to put out a revised edition, consisting only of the front and back covers. It was remaindered within minutes.

The Funniest Works of Fiction Ever Written by Jews

Humour is highly subjective, as everyone knows. While one person might read this book and laugh uproariously, another might read it and laugh uncontrollably. Nevertheless, the results of a survey of over one thousand teachers of world literature have displayed some consensus.

1 The Tevya stories of Sholom Aleichem.
2 *Portnoy's Complaint*, by Philip Roth.
3 *Only in America*, by Harry Golden.
4 *Catch-22*, by Joseph Heller.
5 *The Constitution of the U.S.S.R.*, by a dozen old Jewish Bolsheviks.

III
Israel—Home Free

Great Inventions Which Have Come Out of the Jewish State

Since its founding in 1948, the State of Israel has been a great source of pride, love, and expense for Jews around the world. Among the inventions which have brought the most honour to world Jewry:

The Square Jaffa Orange. After fifty years of research, begun in Florida and concluded in Petach Tikvah, Tzvi Ben-Gog finally managed to invent a hybrid Jaffa orange, which is perfectly square. Easy to cut and easy to peel, the square Jaffa has the crucial advantage of EEP, or Economical Export Packability—an extra two dozen can be fitted snugly into the average crate. Among its few minor flaws, the Square Jaffa Orange tastes like a prune.

The Successful Crossing of an Octopus and a Chicken, performed at the Weizman Institute of Science by Yitzchok Varshawsky, has recently been declared kosher by the Chief Rabbinate of Israel. The octo-chick, only dreamt of by our three forefathers and fantasized about by our four mothers, provides eight legs from each chicken.

Frozen Band-Aids. This incredible breakthrough in medical technology is the creation of Ezra ("Doc") ben Ezra of Natanya. The Frozen Band-Aid, which remains cold even in a heated medicine cabinet, not only soothes cuts and shallow wounds, but has been used successfully to hold together wilting cold cuts at Hadassah luncheons across North America.

The Most Unusual Stamps Issued
by the State of Israel

Philatelists, and even fatalists, from around the world have long rejoiced at the handsome and often stunningly beautiful stamps issued by the Jewish State since its founding. Among the most unusual stamps produced over the past generation are the following:

Special Issue stamp, 2 Lira, commemorating the polite bus queue; Tel Aviv, 1969.

Special Issue stamp, 50 grush, commemorating the occasion of the Great Snow Storm of 1950.

Special Issue stamp, 5 grush, commemorating the Camp David Accords of 1978.

The Best Excuses for Not Making Aliyah

Living in the Land of Israel is considered to be one of the major commandments of the Bible. More laws can be fulfilled there, for one thing; the weather is good, too, as are the dairy products and honey. However, not all Jews *have* "made Aliyah," as one can plainly see. But then, Jewish creativity and powers of rationalization are also well known.

1 "I can give more to the United Jewish Appeal, living in Norfolk."
2 "Self-fulfilment."
3 "I could *never* leave my dear old uncle Charlie, who is such a great guy, not to mention my boss."
4 "There are ninety-nine per cent fewer Arabs here in Des Moines."
5 "My mother would be worried sick."
6 "My mother would *not* worry."
7 "There's so much more I can do for the Jews over here."
8 "If I moved to Israel, then where the hell would I take Irv to have his Bar Mitzvah? Oak Park?"

The Most Incompetent Israeli Tour Guide

Israeli Tour Guides are a species unto themselves, thank God. Otherwise, they might mix with the rest of the Jews and this would be catastrophic to their gene pool.

David "Dudu" Osem (formerly Osterman) of Tel Aviv set new records for creative incompetence on a special tour, consisting of 128 people, which he led on behalf of the Zionist Federation of New Orleans. Mr. Osem:

- booked all thirty-six couples who were strictly kosher into a non-kosher hotel;
- booked the major tour of the Negev for a Saturday morning, when fully one-third of the group would not travel on the Sabbath;

- splashed the eyes of over a dozen men and women who were risking a brief wade in the Dead Sea, nearly blinding them for life and necessitating their hospitalization;
- booked a climb of Mount Masada on the day correctly forecast to be the hottest of the year (144 degrees Fahrenheit);
- led the entire group accidentally across the border into Syria, where they were captured and held for over six months.

Mr. Osem now drives an Egged bus in Jerusalem, where he can do even more damage—daily.

Famous Non-Meetings of Famous Jews

Taking liberties with history is usually a dangerous task. But not in a book like this which in no way claims to be factually or historically accurate.

It is well known (by those who know) that Sigmund Freud, the brilliant founder of psychoanalysis, and Theodor Herzl, who brought about the founding of the Jewish State, both lived near each other in Vienna in the closing years of the nineteenth century. Though they never actually met, the following would undoubtedly have been the essence of their conversation had they done so:

FREUD: So what's your hurry, Mr. Herzl? Why are you fidgeting all over the couch? You'll wear it out.

HERZL: It's not a question of mere "hurrying," Dr. Freud. I must create the Jewish State.

FREUD: What *create* the Jewish state? You are *living* the classic Jewish state: neurosis, anxiety, tension . . .

HERZL: Neurosis? Look, Doctor, people are out to kill the Jews!

FREUD (writing): Uh-hmmmmm. Paranoia.

HERZL: Paranoia!! Everywhere across Europe, people are attacking Jews. Look at the Dreyfus case!

FREUD: I see, I see. Paranoia is when you *think* someone is out to harm you; *Jewish* paranoia is when you *know* someone is out to harm you.

HERZL (sitting up): That's it, Doctor!

FREUD: Really, Teddy. Founding a Jewish State in Palestine—it's madness! I think you need help, lots of help.

(Loud hammering at door; shouts from outside: "Down with the Jews!!")

FREUD: Maybe you'll accept a donation to the cause?

HERZL: Thank you, Doctor. Now you'll be able to say that you really *did* give at the office. Tell me, is there a back entrance to this place?

The Most Common Answers Given by Israelis to the Question, "How long are you here for, in North America?"

The problem of *Yerida* (in other words, leaving Israel to live in other countries) has reached monumental proportions. Inflation, constant war—there are many reasons, and one cannot pass judgment on those Israelis who choose to live in lands other than the Holy One. But one can admire their honesty.

1 "I'm just visiting cousins."
2 "Just until I finish my thesis."
3 "Just until I make my first million."
4 "Until I save up enough money to be able to buy an apartment in Jerusalem." (see No. 3)
5 "Until I get my own taxicab licence."
6 "I've always wanted to experience winter."
7 "Until I learn to ski."
8 "Until I become a professional skier."
9 "Until I become an Olympic skier."

IV
Philanthropy
(and the High Cost of Giving)

The Most Persistent United Jewish Appeal Solicitors

To most North American Jews, the United Jewish Appeal reminds them of death and taxes, except the UJA comes more frequently and is more certain. Millions have given, thousands have collected. But who were the most persistent?

1   Lou Schonfeld broke *in* to the maximum security prison near Fargo, North Dakota, to obtain the pledge from Arthur Stroob, who had just been sentenced to fourteen years for embezzlement and fraud.

2   Walter Jackson (*né* Jacobson) flew to the Bahamas in November, 1977, donned skin-diving equipment, and hit Charles Bieber of Hyde Park, New York, underwater for a $35,000 pledge. It was only two minutes after his oxygen ran out that the New York financier gave in to Jackson's demands.

3   Hyman Leipziger, of Boston, chartered a two-engine plane on March 14, 1989, to search for the person/remains of Irving Macht, a prominent businessman of the same city whose plane had disappeared over the Northwest Territories three days earlier. Macht, frostbitten and near death, was not allowed to board Leipziger's plane until he agreed to a $100,000 donation to the UJA. In the hospital in Yellowknife, Macht was later quoted as saying: "I would not have lighted the flares had I suspected that the plane carried Leipziger."

Little-known Jewish Charities

Charities. Jewish charities. Jewish donors to Jewish charities. Words which go together like milk and honey, Groucho and Chico, love and guilt. The classic Jewish charities that immediately spring to mind are the State of Israel, Jewish Old Folks' Homes, and the Jerry Lewis Telethon. But there are others.

> The Jewish Home for the Chronically Strange in Whitney Pier, Nova Scotia, founded by Abel Kress on December 10, 1922.

> The Jewish Fund for the Morally Handicapped of Mobile, Alabama, founded by Oscar Kaplansky in 1947.

> The Jewish Society for Extended Adolescence of Oakland, California, founded in 1959 by Al Geffen.

Discredited Jewish Fund-raising Techniques

For many reasons—three millennia of concern for the widow and orphan, actual Divine command, guilt over treatment of his mother—the Jew is justifiably famous for charitable donations. Even the poorest Jew is required to give to charity, and usually does. The problem is that not *every* Jew is generous, either by nature or because of fear of the Lord. As they say, "A fool and his money are soon parted," and many Jews do not want to be considered foolish. This lamentable stubbornness has led to some interesting, though discredited, fund-raising techniques used by Jews on Jews:

1 "Hello, Dr. _____? This is _____. You don't know me, but I knew your father, _____, may he rest in peace. Even when he didn't have a pot to spit in, he would give ten, fifteen, even twenty per cent of his earnings to our synagogue's Benevolent Fund. When I think of how his

son, the hot-shot doctor, gives less than ____ per cent of his vastly-higher earnings to charity, I want to throw up. It is said, Doctor, that the dead intercede for the living when they need help. In your case, I think you can forget about the assistance of your revered father, _____."

2   (A WOMAN'S VOICE, YOUNG AND SULTRY) "Hello, Mr._____? Remember me? You helped me with my suitcase at the airport, some months ago. You married? Oh, too bad. You fool around? Great. Why don't we meet next week, at _____, for a drink?"
(THE FOLLOWING WEEK AT THE APPOINTED TIME, THE FUND-RAISER, WITH PHOTOGRAPHER IN TOW, MEETS THE PROSPEC-TIVE PHILANDERER AND SUGGESTS THAT HE TRIPLE HIS DONATION TO THE CHARITY AT HAND.)

3   "Hello? Is this _____, who gave a lousy $____ last year to the Jewish Old Folks' Home Building Fund? Well if you want to see your children _____ and _____ again, leave $_____, in unmarked bills, at the corner of _____ and _____ before midnight tomorrow. God bless you."

The Most Donor Plaques per Square Foot

The use of donor plaques is not limited to Jews, of course: concert halls, theatres, and even museums have wall plaques commemorating people who have donated money to the cause. But the Jews, as in so many things, have tended to go overboard with donor plaques.

The Bais Yaacov Girls High School of Bemidji, Minnesota, has a locker room next to its gymnasium where there are donor plaques on every single locker (116 of them), donor plaques on each shower (12), donor plaques on all 5 hair dryers, and on more than 200 shampoo bottles.

In White Sulphur Springs, West Virginia, in 1969, the Lubavitch Hassidic School of Higher Learning was built entirely out of donor plaques—all four walls, every door, the floors, the roof. Tragically, the building collapsed on January 15, 1970, when a student, Yoshe Kelb, yanked off a donor plaque that had been paid for by a hated uncle. The plaque was at the base of a supporting beam.

V
Jewish History
(Ancient, Modern and Sometimes Even Tolerable)

Reconstruction of the First search for the Lost Tribes of Israel / DShaw '82.

The Earliest Jewish Traffic Signs

Social historians have traced back early traffic laws to England in the sixteenth century but, for some reason, no further. Had they pursued their research as conscientiously as did the authors of this book, they too would have uncovered wayside stones and markers bearing the following inscriptions:

1   *Let There Be Light, Ahead,* an ancient sign believed to be some 5,750 years old, from ancient Mesopotamia.

2   *Slippery When Wet* is the inscription on thousands of stones found throughout the Middle East. Many of the inscriptions are worn away, and the stones themselves smooth and rounded, as if they have been carried along by a great flood.

3   *Caution: Hebrew Crossing* is an ancient sign, dating from Mesolithic Egypt. Whether it was put up by the Pharaoh to assist Hebrew slaves in crossing a busy intersection, or was placed near the Red Sea by some smart-aleck Jews as a gag, will never be known.

4   *Danger, Soft Shoulder* was a traffic sign recently discovered in Gaza; on the back was scrawled the graffito: "Be wary of Delilah's, especially."

The Oldest Jewish Notes

Notes, comments, suggestions—those little jottings of life which so often capture the mood or experiences of a people. Everyone knows of the notes scratched on the walls of caves, which Jews never lived in since they couldn't get anyone to do floors and walls. But there *have* been numerous Jewish notes, starting from many thousands of years ago.

1   *I **know** we all have to make sacrifices, but this is ridiculous,* found scrawled on an altar, probably by Isaac, son of Abraham.

2   *This is the pits,* found on the bottom of a pit, thought to have been scratched out by Joseph, son of Jacob.

3   *Pharaoh is a dummy,* etched into the side of a pyramid, signed "M."

4   *Manna, quail, manna, quail, manna, quail! At least in Egypt we had some **variety!*** found on a papyrus in the Sinai desert, obviously written by an Israelite *kvetch* during the Exodus.

The Most Courageous Speeches Given by Jews

Heroes. What passion and admiration that word inspires. What torture and slaughter that word inspires! Through meticulous research, we have uncovered the eloquent words of some previously ignored Jewish heroes.

1   *How **dare** you call the Jewish people that! Who the hell do you think you **are?*** Bernard ben Gamliel furiously demanded of Antiochus, the Greek-Syrian ruler, in 165 B.C.E. After Antiochus introduced himself to Bernard ben Gamliel, the great scholar tried to take his courageous speech back, but it was too late.

2   *Oh, yeah? You and what army?* was the defiant challenge given by Ephraim ben Joseph to the General of the Roman Army stationed in Jerusalem, 70 C.E. Seconds later, Ephraim ben Joseph saw the army and tried to take his courageous speech back, but it was too late.

3   *Crusades or **no** crusades, get your stupid men off my lawn!* cried Ezekiel Maimon of Hebron, in 1099, to the leader of the ten thousand men who had stopped at his fruit stand to ask directions to Jerusalem. Although the men *were* stupid, proving Ezekiel Maimon correct, and they *did* get off his lawn, proving the power of his courageous speech, there *was* a crusade, which proved distressing to Maimon and everyone else who lived in Palestine at the time.

Famous Last Words of Jewish Heroes

See *The Most Courageous Speeches Given by Jews.*

The Seven Wonders of the Ancient Jewish World

The Hanging Gardens of Babylon, the Colossus of Rhodes, the Pyramid of Cheops. Big deal. The Jews had their own.

1   The birth of Isaac, late in the life of Abraham and his beloved wife, Sarah. Abraham was 100; Sarah was 90. You had to be there.

2   The rise of Joseph to leadership second only to the Pharaoh of Egypt. The thought of a little Jewish kid—one of only a few dozen Jews in the entire world at that time—rising to the top of what was the most gentile nation on earth continues to give pride to Jews, right down to this day.

3   Moses' successful leadership of the ancient Israelites out of the land of bondage. Not only did he have no Jewish education, but he had a bad stutter to boot!

4   Aaron the High Priest's breastplate. It was gorgeous.

5   Delilah's breasts. They were gorgeous.

6   The Holy Temple in Jerusalem. A magnificent structure, built entirely by Jewish architectural firms. But to obtain High Holiday tickets was murder.

7   The victory of the tiny Maccabean army over the great nation of the Syrian-Greeks, leading to the holiday of Hanukkah. Sadly, there was no United Nations to label the Jews aggressors. But no one has ever said that life is fair.

The Worst Jewish Famines

Famines have occurred on earth since the beginning of time, but there are a number which can be considered particularly relevant to Jews.

The famine of Egypt during the time of Joseph and his Brothers, as reported in the Book of Genesis.

The famine of Rosa Ascherheim in Southfield, Michigan, May 27, 1978. When her son Harold suddenly dropped over on that date with his wife, Jan, and their three children, Huey, Dewey, and Louis Ascherheim, Rosa had only eleven lamb chops in the freezer, along with six capons. She was also down to her last three dozen eggs, two dozen potatoes, a small package of eight tomatoes, and only two heads of lettuce. "A famine! A famine!" Rosa Ascherheim cried, rushing across the street to a 7-Eleven store.

Great Jewish Battles

Although fighting and killing have never been way up on the list of Jewish interests (about #193 on a list of 100, we'd say), there have been Jewish battles that have changed the course of history.

The victory of the Maccabees over the Syrian-Greeks, in the second century before the Common Era. Without this battle, the Jews may have died out, and *then* where would Christianity and Islam have been, not to mention Arnold Toynbee, huh?

The battle over the educational upbringing of Jonathan Mirsky, early 1970s, in Brandon, Manitoba. Mr. Mirsky wanted Jonathan to go to public school, so he would learn to relate to the majority faith; Mrs. Mirsky wanted Jonathan to go to a Jewish Day School, so he could know what he would rebel against. The violent stage of the fight ended when Jonathan, then ten years of age, was taken away by court order and placed with a Catholic family. A few months ago, Jonathan met a religious Jewish girl and married her. He is now studying in a *Yeshiva* in New Jersey, which has confused both his biological and adoptive parents totally.

The Lost Tribes of Israel

As every Bible scholar knows and as Sunday School children may have learnt, the Children of Israel were divided into tribes. Only two of these tribes survived over the millennia, and many theories have been put forward about the others—the Falasha of Ethiopia? the American Indians? the New York Islanders? All is conjecture, especially the following list, drawn up for this volume by some of the world's least respected anthropologists.

1 *The Italians*, now primarily Roman Catholic, are probably Jewish in origin, as any visit to New York City will tell you. They use their hands, they sing well, they eat too much, they love show business.

2 *The Greeks*, now mainly Greek Orthodox in faith. They are passionate, drive horribly, and Melina Mercouri has been married to Jules Dassin for years. Need we say more?

3 *The Armenians*. They can't stand the Russians, they love their children, they have names that can't be pronounced, and they have been treated just as poorly over the last century as the Jews have.

4 Probably *Everyone Else in the World* was part of the original lost tribes of Israel, but we are reluctant to point it out to them, for fear of creating anti-Semitism.

The Most Dangerous Jewish Occupations in History

In the Middle Ages, it was a choice of either money-lending or old clothes as Jewish professions, which you have to admit is not much of a choice. In the nineteenth century, it was clothing or the violin. In the twentieth century, it has been clothing or show biz. But that was for only ninety-five per cent of the Jews. What about the remainder, who lived dangerously?

Javelin-catcher at the ancient Greek Olympics. Javelins were not cheap in ancient Greece, but Jewish lives apparently were. For over fifty years, Jews caught javelins, usually in the chest. It was only after one Morris Hebrewopolous complained, that he was informed that the job was javelin-fetcher, not catcher. "*Now* he tells me," said Morris, removing a javelin from his right arm.

Shields in Warfare: Middle Ages. From about 1200 until 1460, Jews were used as shields to protect gentile knights in battle. Jokingly referred to as "Our Shields of David," the Jews considered the job even worse than used clothing sales. "You'd think, with all that experience at javelin-catching back in ancient Greece, they'd be a *lot* better at it," protested King Richard II, Jew in hand, the *mamzer*, he should rot in hell.

Food Taster for the Czar. From 1881 until 1916, Jews were appointed as food tasters for the czars of Russia. Not only was the food often poisoned, but it was also *trefe.* *

---

*And people wonder why so many Russian Jews were Bolsheviks.

The Most Important Groups Founded by Jews

Ever since Joseph's brothers got together and threw their snotty sibling into a ditch, the Jewish people have tended to band together into groups.

1 Christianity
2 The National Association for the Advancement of Colored People (NAACP)
3 The Congress of Racial Equality (CORE)
4 The Student Non-Violent Co-ordinating Committee (SNCC)
5 The Stop the War in Vietnam Action Committee (SWVAC)
6 The Make Franklin Delano Roosevelt King of America Association (MFDRKAA)
7 The Stop Franklin Delano Roosevelt Before He Socializes America Association (SFDRBSAA)
8 The American Civil Liberties Union (ACLU)
9 B'nai B'rith
10 Hadassah

Jewish Coats of Arms

Coats of arms go back to the Middle Ages (or, as Jews warmly call them, the Dark Ages). These designs—with birds, flowers, animals, and so on—were painted on the shields of knights, as well as on their soldiers' uniforms, so the Jews in various European towns would know who was attacking their homes and burning their synagogues. In response, Jews made their *own* coats of arms, the most famous of which are:

1 A slab of lox ascendant and a thick layer of cream cheese on a blue field—the coat of arms of the Mitteranovitch family of Southern France, 1480. What is so astonishing about this coat of arms is that the bagel was not even invented until nearly a century later.

2   A pair of pants couchant, flanked by a giant needle and yellow thread rampant against a green field—the coat of arms of the Schneider family of Alsace-Lorraine, circa 1420.

3   A black beard and *payos* descendent against a black background—the coat of arms of the Plonsker Hassidim, early 1700s. This totally-black coat of arms did not show up well at night, but the Plonsker Hassidim insist that this has saved the lives of their followers on a number of occasions.

The Original, Jewish Names of the Seven Dwarfs

The Seven Dwarfs of fairy tale fame were actually real people who lived in Chelm, Poland, in the eighteenth century. Lack of fresh fruit and vegetables in the town led to the dwindling in height of the Meyerovitch family, who had seven sons. The fame of these boys grew, even if they did not, particularly when they joined a circus that featured the permanently high-flying acrobat, Coca ("Snow") White, of whom they all became enamoured. Miss White's biographer, threatened with a law suit by the strictly orthodox Meyerovitch parents (who certainly didn't want their neighbours to know the seven brothers were hanging around with a *shiksa*), was forced to change the midgets' names when he wrote them into her story. Which is a great pity, for generations of children have had to settle for "Dopey," "Grumpy," and "Sneezy" when they could have relished the poetry of the names:

Fybush
Nissin
Pinchas
Reuven
Shraga
Shabbatai
Zissel

The Earliest Known Jewish Musical Groups

1 "Noah and the Animals" made a world tour, ending in Turkey/Armenia, 3090 before the Common Era.
2 "Morris Citrus and the Fruits," a group of Jewish singers at the Holy Temple in Jerusalem, c. 2200 B.C.E.
3 "The Rock of Ages," formed in 165 B.C.E. by Judah Maccabee and his brothers.
4 "Paul and the Apostles," a Jewish-Christian group, formed in 29 of the Common Era. It ended up being one of the most popular groups in history. Still touring.

Jews Who Have Bought Things Retail

In the more than four thousand years of Jewish existence and survival (and the two things aren't always the same), there is only one known, verified case of a Jew who actually bought things at full price. Indeed, shocking as it may seem, the unrepentant wretch actually wrote about the deed, and even recommended it to others!

Baruch ("Barry" to his close friends) Spinoza, of Amsterdam, Holland (1632–1677), was one of the most important thinkers since the Renaissance. Nevertheless, in his major work, *On the Improvement of Understanding*, Spinoza urged fellow Jews to "shop well; shop carefully; shop around. But always pay the full price. It is unethical to bargain, and all the more unethical to ask for discounts or financial favours."

Spinoza was excommunicated by the rabbinate of Holland. As the Chief Rabbi at the time observed at dinner: "Let him eat pig. Let him intermarry. But surely let him not urge our people to buy retail. The Jews have suffered enough."

The Longest Undiscovered Marrano

The Marranos were Spanish Jews who, during the Inquisition, found it necessary to pass themselves off as Christian. During the fifteenth and sixteenth centuries, many of these Jews emigrated to other lands; many were caught and punished (a euphemism for tortured); still others eventually became Catholics. But not all.

Juan ben Rubinoff Lopez of Saragossa, Spain, was discovered by a UJA canvasser from Fort Wayne, Indiana, on May 2, 1951. Lopez instinctively denied the charge, but could not explain away, to the satisfaction of the UJA, why he had been observed

- mumbling the *Shema* when he entered church each day;
- spitting three times whenever he heard the priest of his local parish tell of the suffering of the Basque peasants;
- lighting eight votive candles in church every December;
- rocking back and forth while at mass;
- hating the taste of liquor;
- placing photos of John Garfield and Tony Curtis all over his bedroom wall;
- inexplicably changing his bedsheets and pillowcases every Friday afternoon, and expressing longings for Chinese food every Saturday night;
- marrying a Jewish girl, which drove his Catholic mother crazy.

"The Inquisition had nothing on you guys," a defeated and bitter Lopez remarked.

Actions Which Can Predict the Coming
of the Messiah

Unlike another major world religion, which will remain name-less, the Jews are still waiting for their messiah. Will he come on the back of a donkey, some ask. Will he come in a Mercedes-Benz? No one knows. But if any of the following events take place, then—as sure as the sun will rise tomorrow—the Messiah will most assuredly come.

When one million Jewish women remove the plastic slip covers from their living room sofas and chairs.

When grandmothers of the Jewish faith refuse to feed their grandchildren.

When mothers of the Jewish faith refuse to over-feed their children.

When Jewish men as well as women do not ask other Jewish men and women whether or not they have unmarried sons and daughters.

VI
Synagogues,
Rabbis, Cantors
(and Other Mixed Blessings)

The Shortest Jewish Sermons

Long sermons are, as we all know, a little taste of hell on earth. Even excellent long sermons are too long. We therefore acknowledge, and praise, the record-breaking *short* sermons given by rabbis.

1   Rabbi Eliezer ben Yosef spoke on "The Evils of Rome" to a congregation in Rome, Italy, in the year 45. At the two-minute point in his sermon, two dozen centurions rushed up to the pulpit and gave the unfortunate rabbi some examples of Roman evil.

2   "Why We Should Support the Mensheviks," a didactic sermon given by Rabbi Yisroel Rabinowitz in Moscow on November 10, 1917. Approximately eight minutes into the sermon, a group of Bolsheviks rose up from the front row of the synagogue and carried the rabbi off.

3   "The Dangers of Adultery," a passionate talk on the importance of marital fidelity, was given by Rabbi Michael Stern in Winnipeg, Manitoba. After nine minutes and twenty seconds, his wife, Shirley, leapt up and attacked the rabbi with both fists, driving him from the synagogue. She felt that he had done too much research on the topic.

The Longest Sermons Delivered in a Synagogue

There will be no introduction to this list of record sermons. They were long enough, as it is.

1 Rabbi Harvey Srebnick of Temple B'nai Kesef, Boston, spoke for 1 hour, 47 minutes on "The Contemporary Implications of Aaron the High Priest's Breastplate," March 5, 1966. His life-time contract was broken by his congregation the following Monday, leading to lengthy litigation (see *Famous Jewish Court Cases*).

2 Rabbi Yossel Borochov of Lodz, Poland, expounded for 3 hours, 1 minute on the importance of not eating meat torn from living animals; November 29, 1901. By the end of the second hour of his talk, there was a massive migration of his congregation to the United States and Canada.

3 Fidel Castro, guest speaker at Shaarey Siesta Congregation in Havana, Cuba, explained in detail for 8 hours, 14 minutes his new Five-Year plan and its relevance to the Jews; January 8, 1961. Only one person walked out, at hour 6—Jacobo Agronowitz. He was never heard from nor seen again.

The Strangest Titles of Jewish Sermons

Are the Jews "strange"? Many people have thought so. But, on the whole, not half as strange as some of their rabbis.

1 "The Sermon on the Mounties," a talk on the place of the Royal Canadian Mounted Police in the lives of Jewish Montrealers; in Lachine, Quebec, June 1, 1965, by Rabbi Eli Fenekal.

2 "Why the President of our Synagogue Is a *Mamzer*," the final sermon given by Rabbi Jacob Kurzweill of Temple Ain Sholom of Great Neck, New York. The rabbi had just learnt that the board was refusing him a life-time contract.

3 "Sex and the Single Rabbi," a sermon by Rabbi David Sklare at Congregation B'nai Bat, Washington, D.C., after the thirtieth attempt to fix him up with a daughter of a congregant.

The Worst Faux Pas Made at a Jewish Funeral

Funerals are distressing experiences for everyone, with the possible exception of funeral directors. It is with sadness, then, that we list the two worst faux pas ever made at the funeral of a Jew, may he rest in peace.

1 At the burial of Jake Leventhal of Portland, Oregon, the rabbi repeatedly referred to the deceased as "Murray," and praised his excellence with his hands, when everyone knew that Jake Leventhal could barely tie his own shoelaces without throwing a temper tantrum.

2 More than three dozen people shook the hand of Hilda Leventhal, bemoaning the loss of "your dear Murray," and commenting on how gifted he was with his hands; Portland, Oregon.

The Shortest Tenure of a Jewish Rabbi

How long should the contract of a rabbi be? Two years? Five years? Seven pages? Next to the exact date when the Messiah will come, this is the most agonizing question ever confronted by Jews.

1   Rabbi Yossel Meisel of North Bay, Ontario, was fired twenty-four minutes after he signed a five-year contract at Beth Grepz, when he was asked in passing what he would be speaking on, that coming Sabbath, and replied, in astonishment: "*What*? It's bad enough that I have to bury people and marry people, but you want I should work on *Shabbos*, **too**?"

2   Rabbi Bernard Landsberger of Toledo, Ohio, was fired about seventeen hours after he signed a two-year contract with the board of Congregation Shaarey Weinstock of Toledo. The orthodox elders of the synagogue threw Rabbi Landsberger out when he entered the Sabbath services in blue jeans and T-shirt, smoking a cigarette. Afterwards, the aggrieved rabbi stated: "I keep kosher. I pray three times a day. I call my mother regularly. They never asked me about my dress code and any bad habits, and I didn't offer."

3   Rabbi Avraham Kippletsky of Congregation Anshe Poland, of Tallahassee, Florida, resigned his position on the first Sabbath after he had signed his ten-year contract. He was affronted when he entered the house of worship and saw all the board members in blue jeans and T-shirts. "I don't need his kind of 'holier than thou' attitude," said President of the Board Adam Cousins. "At least we don't *smoke*."

The Shortest Tenure of a Cantor

Hazzanim, who lead the congregational prayers, have traditionally found it difficult to remain on good terms with their boards of directors. A complete list of short-lived appointments would be extremely long; certainly longer than their tenures. Here, though, are some record-holders:

1   Cantor Herzl Teitelbaum of Rattlesnake, Wyoming (Temple B'nai Frum), was fired on the very first Sabbath he sang. He held out the "Mussaf Kedushah" for thirty-seven minutes, a prayer for which four minutes normally suffices. Since the congregants have to stand during this holy prayer, and since the temperature was 106 degrees Fahrenheit, hundreds of members of the Temple collapsed and fainted. Fortunately, there were still enough men and women conscious at the end of the service to bodily remove the cantor from the building and drag him to the bus station.

    "Did they hire me to sing, or to *kibbitz*?" asked Teitelbaum angrily, as his bus pulled into Chicago. "When I'm paid to sing, I *sing*."

2   Cantor Siegmund Fuchtwang of Edmonton, Alberta, had his contract torn up by the president of the board of Congregation Beth Assimilation less than five minutes after he had signed a five-year deal. It seems that someone on the board invited Cantor Fuchtwang to lead the group of men in a song to celebrate his new job, and he sang miserably off-key. Said the outraged cantor in court, a few months later: "They offer me a lousy $500-a-month contract, and they expect a good voice in the bargain?"

The Largest Synagogue in the World

Although there have been many contenders, the largest single synagogue or temple in modern history is clearly Temple Beth Zoftig of Green Bay, Wisconsin.

Over 2,000 feet long and 2,500 feet wide, the temple can seat 45,000 people, and even more during the High Holidays. Since the Jewish community of Green Bay is rather small, the synagogue board rents out the building to the Green Bay Packers football team, which practises inside the temple in inclement weather.

From the back of the structure, it is impossible to see the rabbi or hear the choir. According to most members, this is one of the chief attractions of belonging to Temple Beth Zoftig.

The Smallest Synagogue

In spite of the incredible size of many North American synagogues (which, according to one architecture critic, suffer from an "edifice complex") the Jews have traditionally prayed in structures that were not impressive. This was partially due to extreme poverty in Eastern Europe, and occasionally the result of the Islamic order that no building could be taller than a mosque. But there were some which were *really* small.

The smallest known synagogue on earth was the Sheyg *shul*, in the Polish community of the same name. Built in 1887 with the left-over wood from a *Sukkah*, the *shul* was large enough for only three people to pray in comfortably. This was a distinct disadvantage when it came to reciting those prayers and services that require a *minyan*.

The yearly membership was the equivalent of only five cents in 1982 money, which was still far more than the average Jew of Sheyg, Poland, could afford, anyway.

Most of the Jews of the town were pleased with the Sheyg *shul* despite its tiny size, because no one could tolerate the rabbi, Dov-Ber Fleishhacker, and according to the president of the Sheyg *shul* board, the rabbi's wife was no bargain, either.

The Worst Names of Synagogues

What's in a name? In the case of the average North American Jew not too much, since most of their parents changed theirs when they came over to the New World, anyway. Synagogues have traditionally been named after Biblical injunctions or images: Shomrai Shabbos, Shaaray Shomayim, Beth Sholom. Some have more distinctive names, however.

1   Saint Christopher Street Shul, Peterborough, Ontario.

2   Anshe Dixie, Atlanta, Georgia.

3   Congregation Temple Beth Israel Am B'nai Torah Anshe Sholom Tzedek Hillel Shaarei Titus, an amalgamation of several synagogues that went under; Chicago and environs, Illinois.

4   Our Lady of Perpetual Mercy and Guilt, a building shared by a Catholic Church and a Reform Temple on Long Island, New York.

The Highest Bima

Having an *aliya* is considered a great honour to Jews, and it has often been paid for with a donation to charity. Some synagogues take the word *aliyah* very literally.

1   Temple Anshe Denver in Denver, Colorado, was built on the side of one of the Rocky Mountains. To have an *aliya* there entails the use of oxygen mask and pitons, as one climbs the craggy sides of the *bimah*. In over a quarter-century of use, the synagogue has reported only three injuries during Torah readings: one caused by a faulty piton during an elderly man's rappel; and two cases of hypoxia when the oxygen masks were temporarily removed to recite the blessings.

2   Temple Ohev Shomayim in the Carpathians, in Eastern Europe (the town changed countries so much, no one cared any more which country it belonged to). At this temple, the first known escalator was installed in the 1920s so that elderly Jews could reach the *bimah* with ease. Unfortunately, the vast majority of the worshippers were extremely religious, so they refused to use the electrically-operated escalator on the Sabbath and holy days. The *shul* went defunct in 1928.

The Most Common Lines from Bar Mitzvah Speeches

1   "The first candle will be lit by . . ."
2   "Today I am a man, no matter *what* my mother says."
3   "If only my Uncle Yitz could be here . . ."
4   "I'd like to thank my teachers, without whose persistence and tone deafness . . ."
5   "Today I am an Israeli bond."
6   "If the band could stop playing already, I'd like to thank . . ."
7   "Unaccustomed as I am to public speaking . . ."
8   "I'd like to thank Dad for that roasting of his only son. But seriously, folks . . ."
9   "I'm especially flattered that my Aunt _____ is here, all the way from _____ ."
10 "It's a great thrill to finally be Bar Mitvahed, because now I can finally drop out of Hebrew school and play in the little league like the other kids in the seventh grade."
11 "I can hardly wait to get home and see what's in these envelopes so many of you have handed me."

The Highest Temperature in a Synagogue Where a Woman Wore a Mink Stole

"When you've got it, flaunt it." So said Rabbi Moshe Zekaynim the Elder, in ancient Minos. Many modern Jews agree.

118 degrees Fahrenheit, at Temple Beth Retired in Phoenix, Arizona, August 24, 1980. When the air-conditioning blew early in the Sabbath morning service, Mrs. Rose Warson (originally of Calgary, Alberta) refused to take off her stole. She came to, three days later in the Mt. Carmel Hospital, weighing thirteen pounds less than she had weighed on that fateful Sabbath morning.*

The Most Expensive High Holiday Tickets Not Used

As is well known, the Jewish High Holidays of Rosh Hashana and Yom Kippur are so faithfully observed, even by the least religious Jew, that most congregations find it necessary to sell tickets to participants, even if they are already members. But not all people get to use their tickets.

Max Reissner of Castro Valley, California, paid $500 for a single seat near the front of Temple New Voriche for the Jewish High Holidays, September,1989. He put the ticket in his wallet, and did not come across it until October 30, three weeks after Yom Kippur was past. "I don't know Hebrew anyway," said Mr. Reissner, "and the rabbi is second-rate. But my gentile friends would never speak to me if I didn't at least *try* to *go* to *shul* on the holidays."

*Mrs. Warson is the author of the current bestseller *The Phoenix Diet*, excerpted in the *National Enquirer* and the *New York Times*.

The Best Tunes for "Adon Olam"

There are many miracles in Judaism: the splitting of the Red Sea; the sun standing still for Joshua; Empire Chicken in the frozen foods section. But the ultimate miracle is how the words of "Adon Olam," the closing hymn of Sabbath morning services, seem to fit every tune on earth.

1   "Turkey in the Straw"
2   Mahler's Eighth Symphony (second movement)
3   "Come to Me My Melancholy Baby"
4   Bruce Springsteen's "Born to Run"
5   "(I Did It) My Way"
6   "The Star-spangled Banner"
7   The Beatles' "A Day in the Life"
8   The "Internationale"
9   Rod Stewart's "Do You Think I'm Sexy?"
10 "Ebb Tide"
11 George Burns's "How Could You Believe Me When I Said I Loved You When You Know I've Been a Liar All My Life?"
12 The Rolling Stones' "(I Can't Get No) Satisfaction"
13 "You Deserve a Break Today (at McDonald's)"
14 "The Jet Song" from *West Side Story*
15 "When the Saints Go Marching In"
16 Madonna's "Like a Prayer"

The Most Successful "Alternative Minyans"

Since the 1960s, more and more Jews in North America and around the world have tried to start their own alternative *minyans*, or services. These groups of Jews wish to pray together without the formal encumbrances of synagogue walls and other concerns. Although there have been many hundreds of these groups, three stand out as being worthy of mention:

1   The West Side Minyan, formed on the West Bank (alias "the Liberated Territories") of the Jordan River after the Six Day

War of 1967. Originally composed of thirty-six Israeli men and women, it has now dwindled to a bare minimum—ten men. Of the other twenty-six, three have moved to Waltham, Massachusetts, to study the demography of Israel from the outside, and the other twenty-three are driving cabs in New York City, studying the Decline of the West from the inside.

2   The East Side Minyan of Manhattan, formed in 1978, consists mainly of former Israelis who drive cabs in New York.

3   The Supply Side Minyan, formed by Ronald Reagan in January of 1981 in Washington, D.C. It consists of Republicans of the Jewish faith who sit for hours every Sabbath, reading The Gospel according to David Stockman.

The Most Miserly Kiddish Given by a Jew

The tradition of giving a *kiddish*—wine, food, snacks—after a religious service, in honour or in memory of someone, is a long and pleasant one, which is why we are mortified to record the following:

1 Tam-Tam   no napkins
1 piece herring   no toothpicks
1 kichel   3 wet chick peas

at Congregation B'nai Pasgoodnik, Victoria, British Columbia; June 1, 1955.

The Least Self-conscious Man at a Sabbath Kiddish

Nachum Pomerantz of Montreal, Quebec, who was visiting Congregation B'nai Pasgoodnik of Victoria on June 1, 1955, and who ate:

1 Tam-Tam   1 kichel
1 piece herring   3 chick peas

VII
Jewish Rituals
(and Other Things
to Rebel Against)

The Sloppiest Bris in History

The Jewish ritual circumcision is one of the most ancient commandments of our people, dating from the time of Abraham, the first Jew, who learned that circumcision as an adult is no treat, let me tell you. Naturally, over four thousand years, some records for irreversible clumsiness have been set:

1   The Circumcision of Shimon Levi Benjamin in Vilna, Lithuania, on January 6, 1911, by "Three-fingers" Jacobson, *né* "Five-fingers" Jacobson, the *mohel* of the unfortunate community. Until the January 6th circumcision, he had been known as "Four-fingers" Jacobson.

2   The Circumcision of Harriet Weinstock, *née* Harry Weinstock, performed on May 28, 1971 by a *mohel* who wishes to remain nameless until the court case is complete.

The Fastest Ritual Circumcision
of a Jewish Child

The *bris* is central to Jewish existence. But central or not, there have been times when the Jews were in a hurry.

1 Dr. Reuven Kass of Toronto, Ontario, circumcized a Jewish baby in only 18.3 seconds, using an electric carving knife, on March 2, 1970.

2 Dr. Reuven Kass of Toronto, Ontario, circumsized another Jewish baby in 14.1 seconds, using a Cuisinart, on June 16, 1978.

3 Rabbi Maury Henkowitz of Seattle, Washington, during a commercial break in the Dodgers/Oakland World Series, circumcized a Jewish male in exactly 59 seconds on October 28, 1988.

Songs Traditionally Sung
at Ritual Circumcisions

Tens of millions of Jewish children, preferably boys, have undergone the moving religious experience of a *bris*. Over the years, understandably, many tunes have become associated with this observance. The most common include:

1 "I've Got You Under My Skin"
2 "All of Me, Why Not Take All of Me"
3 "(Oh, No) They Can't Take That Away from Me"
4 "The First Cut Is the Deepest"

Note: In the late 1970s, an extremely unpopular *mohel* from Ogden, Utah, used to begin all *brises* humming Meatloaf's popular hit, "Two Out of Three Ain't Bad."

The Hardest Jewish Puzzle in History

The following picture puzzle, invented by Dr. Chaim Salkowitz of New York City to test the Jewish knowledge of graduates of Jewish day schools of the United States, fooled over seventy-eight per cent of the ten thousand Jewish children who tried it. See how well *you* do:

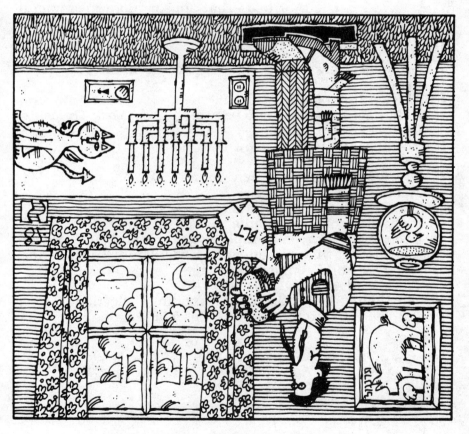

What's Wrong with This Picture?

In the drawing above, there are a number of things that are not correct. Can you find 10?

The Most Commonly Used Texts for "Creative" Jewish Weddings

The Jews, like other people, have often longed to have more "interesting" weddings than their parents and ancestors. However, tying the knot while jumping from a plane, or getting married underwater, is not at all the Jewish way; instead, many have searched for texts that appear more meaningful than the traditional one.

1. Dostoyevsky's *The Idiot*.
2. Groucho Marx attacking Margaret Dumont in *Horse Feathers*.
3. The writings of Kahlil Gibran.
4. Editorials from the Op-Ed page of the *New York Times*.
5. Lyrics by John Lennon.
6. Readings from Fran Lebowitz.
7. Poems by Rod McKuen.
8. Great exchanges between Johnny Carson and Ed McMahon.
9. The Thoughts of Chairman Mao.
10. Richard Nixon's resignation speech.
11. Exchanges between Humphrey Bogart and Lauren Bacall (the latter of whom is, after all, Jewish) from *To Have and Have Not* and *Key Largo*.
12. *The World According to Garp*.
13. The Hallmark Greeting Cards Wedding Collection.
14. Putdowns by Archie Bunker to his wife, Edith.

The Most Popular Songs Played at Jewish Weddings

Millennia of weddings have led to a rash of songs which Jews love to hear as the bride and groom dance happily about the room. In 1980, a survey was taken across North America, and it was found that the following were the songs most frequently played at Jewish weddings:

1   "If I Were a Rich Man" from *Fiddler on the Roof.*
2   "Matchmaker, Matchmaker" from *Fiddler on the Roof.*
3   The title song from *Fame.*
4   "To Dream the Impossible Dream" from *Man of La Mancha.*
5   "Maria" from *West Side Story.*
6   The theme from *The Godfather.*
7   "Tradition" from *Fiddler on the Roof.*
8   "The Wedding March" from *Lohengrin*, by Richard Wagner.
9   "(You say you want) A Revolution" by The Beatles.
10 "Bye, Bye, Miss American Pie."

For other favourites, see the list of Hassidic lyrics on page 17.

The Classiest Conclusion of a Jewish Wedding Ceremony

The Jewish wedding ceremony is much loved, if only because it lasts a mere ten minutes or so. Other than that, many feel there's not much to be said for it. But even with such a brief ceremony, some pretty classy people have been able to endow it with special significance.

1 Nat Sokolow of Norfolk, Virginia, used a Steuben glass to break under his foot in the traditional ending of the Jewish wedding ceremony. The hand-cut crystal was worth over $2,400. His wife of ten seconds, Shirley Appleton, promptly divorced him for his ridiculous extravagance.

2 Albert Fishbine of Montreal, Quebec, movingly toasted his new bride with a family *kiddish* cup. Rare and hand-blown, the glass cup had been designed and made in Lithuania, and had been handed down through his wife's family for six generations. In a flamboyant gesture, Mr. Fishbine then threw the cup over his shoulder, shattering it and his new mother-in-law's feelings simultaneously. His mother-in-law never spoke to him again, and the couple enjoyed over twenty happy years of marriage as a result.

The Most Vulgar Jewish Funerals

Jews are renowned for their good taste. But there are exceptions to everything.

1   At the uproarious funeral of Herb Weinstock of Beverly Hills, California, one dozen large TVs hooked up with video-cassette recorders hung from the ceiling of the funeral home, displaying Herb, taped three years earlier, smoking a long cigar and telling incredibly filthy jokes.

2   Art Freifeld, the multi-millionaire of Fredericton, New Brunswick, had requested that his will be read at the grave-side. This guaranteed not only that a large crowd would show up (something which all his business associates had vowed *not* to do), but also that many of the tears shed would be genuine.

The Shortest Shiva

Psychologists of every faith have admired the Jewish *shiva*, in the way this ritual allows the mourner to come to grips with his or her loss, surrounded by loved ones. But not every Jew has sat for the full seven days.

Ethel Sterling, upon the burial of her husband, Julius, looked about the gathering at the graveside service and shouted, "I couldn't *stand* him for thirty-two years, and I'm not about to *sit* for him now!" She then turned and went off to an afternoon movie with her best friend, Tsippie Cooperman; Philadelphia, 1966.

The Dietary Laws

The dietary laws of the Jews are complex, difficult to observe, and fascinating, not to mention guilt-provoking if they are not kept. Some Jews outdo each other in daring, and have been observed (by observant Jews) with the following:

The Most Trefe Trefe

1   A ham sandwich eaten on Passover.
2   A ham and cheese sandwich, eaten on Passover.
3   A ham and cheese sandwich on rye, eaten on Yom Kippur.
4   A ham and cheese sandwich on white, eaten on Yom Kippur.
5   A ham and cheese sandwich on white, with mayonnaise, eaten on Yom Kippur.
6   Clam-stuffed veal with Hollandaise sauce—served, wolfed down, and paid for on Yom Kippur.

The Least Trefe

Sour cream with sour cream topping.

**The Most Controversial Food *re* Its Kosher Nature,
in Modern Rabbinics**

1　Sturgeon.
2　Dolphin.
3　Dinner at Hinda Morrison's house since Harold, who was
　the observant one, moved out.

Mitzvot Which All Jews Follow

All faiths suffer from lack of total allegiance of their followers to
their respective precepts. It is unfortunately true that the occasional Jew might taste pork or forget to go to synagogue on the
Sabbath, God forbid. But out of the large number of *mitzvot*
God had given to the Jews, there are a few that are literally
never transgressed by the Jewish people.

1　The king must write a special copy of the Torah for himself.
　　　　　　　　　　　　　　　　　　　　　Deuteronomy, 17:18

2　The high priest may marry only a virgin.
　　　　　　　　　　　　　　　　　　　　　Leviticus, 21:13

3　Cattle to be sacrificed must be at least eight days old and
　without blemish.
　　　　　　　　　　　　　　　　　　　Leviticus, 22:27; 22:21

4　A Nazirite must let his hair grow during the period of his
　separation.
　　　　　　　　　　　　　　　　　　　　　　　Numbers, 6:5

5　The ashes of the red heifer are to be used in the process of
　ritual purification.
　　　　　　　　　　　　　　　　　　　　　　Numbers, 19:2-9

6　A Jewess may not marry an Ammonite or Moabite.
　　　　　　　　　　　　　　　　　　　　　Deuteronomy, 23:4

Little-known Jewish Blessings

Like most religions, Judaism offers blessings before and after meals, blessings to request favours from God, and even blessings that should be made before the doing of a *mitzvah*. But what other religion has *these*?

"Blessed art thou, Lord, king of the universe, . . .

. . . who kept me away from St. Petersburg last Monday, when the cossacks went on a rampage." (Russia, 1882)

. . . who gave me an uncle like Sender Gelman, who made it to Alberta, Canada, and had the decency to send me a ticket to come over." (Budapest/Edmonton, 1928)

. . . for recommending that I go into business with Jack Orlinsky instead of my crooked brother-in-law Sol." (New York City, 1941)

. . . who gives me the strength to cope with the incompetent dealings of my partner, Jack Orlinsky." (New York City, 1946)

. . . who has blessed me with a beautiful daughter who should only meet someone soon because she is eating me and her mother out of house and home." (New York City, 1958)

. . . who found a decent man for my daughter, even though I have a feeling that he is too old for her and is a lousy businessman." (New York City, 1961)

. . . who cursed me with a son-in-law like Jack Orlinsky." (New York City, 1964)

The Fastest Shacharit

A visit to any synagogue on a weekday morning is a sobering experience for anyone who does not know the Hebrew language well.

The modern record for the fastest recital of the *Shacharit* service was set at Congregation Beth David of Raleigh, North Carolina, on May 9, 1989: 4 minutes and 33 seconds. Which is not bad, considering that there are over sixty pages of prayers. The leader of that record service was Cantor Fendel Grauman, who moonlights as an auctioneer for the Reynolds Tobacco Corporation. Discussing his achievement later in the day, Grauman remarked: "The four-minute mark will be the great psychological barrier for some time to come."

The Yarmulka and Its Derivatives

The *yarmulka* is of such ancient origin that it is only logical to assume that it must have had countless derivatives over thousands and thousands of years. Or so.

1   The beret, invented by French religious Jews who wanted to hide their religiosity and still keep the faith and look *très chic*.

2   The iron helmet was created by Jews of Central Europe who were distressed that their normal yarmulkas did not prevent bullets from entering their heads.

3   The ten-gallon hat was *not* invented by Texans, but by a Jew who wanted to be able to keep his prayer shawl and prayer books on his person, but couldn't carry those things on the Sabbath.

4   The tam-o'-shanter, with its centre tassel, was invented by Polish Jews who, when landing on the shores of Great Britain, wanted to look as Scottish as possible.

The Most Expensive Yarmulkas

Every few years, one hears of auctions of famous people's belongings—Churchill's automobile, a Beatle's guitar, and so on. Jews are no different in valuing the belongings of those who went before them. One case in point is the *yarmulka*. While the average skullcap can cost as much as fifty dollars or more, if made with fine material by a craftsman, it can be as cheap as a half-dozen for a dollar, when it is mass produced for weddings or bar mitzvahs. The high point in the *yarmulka* market was indubitably reached at Sotheby's of London, on April 1, 1981, when the following skullcaps were sold at auction:

1   A skullcap made of white cotton, with the inscription on the inside: "The wedding of Elizabeth Taylor and Mike Todd—Feb. 21, 1957, Mexico." For $550.

2   A skullcap made from potato sack, embroidered with the inscription: "From Eliezer Baal Shem Tov's Bar Mitzvah, March 3, 1673." For $1,080.

3   A papyrus skullcap, bearing the hieroglyph: "This belongs to Moses, on the occasion of the giving of the Ten Commandments." Brought in $55,000.

4   A skullcap of woven silk, with the inscription: "To my beloved Isaac, on his near-sacrifice, from his daddy Abe." Sold for $254,500.

The Weirdest Materials for a Skullcap

Cotton, silk, what else would be necessary? You'll see.

Asbestos, worn by a religious fireman in Tel Aviv, Israel.

Urea-formaldehyde, worn by Evel Knievel's assistant, Joseph "Bones" Lupovitch, in Butte, Montana.

The Most Words and Weirdest Inscriptions on a Yarmulka

1 The first six chapters of the book of Genesis.

2 The Israeli Declaration of Independence.

3 "Eat at Moishe's" (worn by Moishe Penovsky, owner of Moishe's Grill in Queen's, New York).

4 "Software Configuration Management," the title of a book that is not a bestseller by the brother of one of the authors of this book.

5 Two verses plus chorus of "Hatikvah."

6 "Love me, hate me, but don't ignore me." Worn by Ziggie Koppel after he had been rejected by Hannah Eizenbaum of Vancouver, B.C. The *yarmulka* was made by Fran Schumeister, Ziggie's new girl-friend, who swore she would do *anything* to make Ziggie happy.

7 "Come to Me, My Melancholy Baby."

8 "It's hard to be a Jew, and wearing this all the time doesn't make it any easier."

The Longest Payos Worn by a Religious Jew

The *mitzvah* of letting the sidelocks of the hair grow endlessly can be traced back to the Bible. But the record for the longest *payos* can be traced only to this book:

> Yossele Grynspan of Ozerov, Poland, 1874-1935, had earlocks that, according to his friends and many students, were more than eighteen feet long. When in playful mood, such as on Jewish holidays, Reb Yossele would tie the ends together and skip rope.

The Curliest Sidelocks

While religious Jews would often let the sides of their hair grow forever, they would also curl them around their fingers when studying, or thinking, or running for safety.

Asher ben Aryeh of Yemen wound his *payos* more than twenty-three times around his left ear, and nineteen times around his right ear, allowing him to pick up the 1947 World Series from the United States on short wave and long *payos*. Unfortunately, he did not understand a word.

Rabbi Meir Riselman (1848-1904) of Krakow, Poland, used to curl his *payos* absent-mindedly during prayer and study. Once, just before the 1896 pogrom, he had them so taut that when they uncoiled, his body spun about and was thrown over forty yards to safety.

The Most Ostentatious Mezuzah

The *mezuzah*, usually of modest size, has occasionally become a Jewish status symbol. And speaking of California . . .

The "Rabinowicz Masterpiece" is four feet high and five feet wide and flashes the Lord's name in a dozen different languages, once every ten seconds. It stands next to the front door of Max Rabinowicz, the Hollywood producer ("*the* Hollywood producer," he tells us), in Malibu.

The Sexiest Shaytel

The *shaytel* has been worn by strictly orthodox Jewish women for centuries, as a mark of modesty and faithfulness. Which is why we are as shocked as you are at the following:

The sexiest *shaytel* of Eastern Europe belonged to Esther Rifka Zylberschlag of Boryslaw, Poland. Whenever Mrs. Zylberschlag, wearing her strawberry-blonde wig, would step out into the street, the most aged men of the small community would turn their heads away and spit, while the teenaged *yeshiva bochers* would run after her, panting and braying. "You know, Esther Rivka isn't such an attractive woman," her husband once admitted, "but that *shaytel* turns her into quite a looker, doesn't it? To be frank with you, I beg her not to show me her real hair when we're home alone."

The sexiest *shaytel* in the State of Israel is, or rather was, worn by Minnie Fesselman of B'nai Brak. It was so flashy and daring ("Technicolor!" ruled one rabbi at the time) that Mrs. Fesselman was excommunicated by her congregation, and her *shaytel* was confiscated and burned. "It even *burned* sexy," reminisced Mrs. Fesselman, sadly.

The Least-used Bar Mitzvah Gifts

The entries in this category could fill a book in themselves, and it would probably be given as a Bar Mitzvah gift. For this reason, we have decided to limit the following to books on Jewish topics.

1   *Famous Rocks of the Old Testament*, given by Mr. and Mrs. Arnold Rosenberg to their nephew Herbie on the occasion of his Bar Mitzvah; June 10, 1977. Within five days, the book was given, with a new inscription, to Mr. and Mrs. Arnold Rosenberg on the occasion of their twentieth wedding anniversary, by little Herbie's parents, Sol and Betty Rosenberg of Chicago.

2   *Jewish Communists Who Excelled in Polish Sports*, an over-sized and justifiably under-purchased hard cover, was Bobby Silberstein's Bar Mitzvah gift to his childhood friend Daniel Lapidus; Boston, January 29, 1980. The book was thrown out with its wrapping paper, purportedly accidentally, by the family maid on February 1.

3   *March 1328, and Other Happy Months in Jewish History*, a slim volume, was received and promptly misplaced by Benjie Celnik on his Bar Mitzvah day, November 1, 1964. The givers of the gift, Benjie's grandparents Louis and Bertha Orenstein of Denver, over the following five years continually asked how he had enjoyed the book, leading to a complete rift in the family in 1969.

VIII
The Jewish Calendar
(and Other Timely Concerns)

Little-known Jewish Holy Days

Even non-Jews are aware of Passover, Yom Kippur, and various other dates on the Jewish calendar. But, surprisingly, many Jews do not know every single holy day of their own faith. Among the least known:

1 The Burning of the Mortgage of Temple Beth Naar of Seymour, Indiana. The mortgage still had $3.7 million left to pay off, but it went up in flames along with the Temple on March 12, 1979. Police are still investigating. (A feast; maybe a fast.)

2 The Anniversary of Rabbi Moishe ben Mamzer's third divorce. She got the cart, he got to keep the horse. Pinsk (or was it Minsk?), Russia. (A fast.)

3 The Birthday of Meyer Finklestein, who entered university directly from Grade 4, Brooklyn, New York. (A feast, although everyone wonders why; he never amounted to borscht.)

The Best Way to Remember the Jewish Calendar

People have often protested about the awkwardness of the Gregorian (or is it the Julian?) calendar: Why *should* February have 28 days? Why does June have 30, when July has 31? Still, the calendar used by most of the world is a picnic compared with the Jewish calendar, which is based on both the moon *and* the sun. And inserting an extra month 7 times during each 19-year period makes the February 29th dilemma look like cake.

How, then, can Jews remember the Jewish calendar? By memorizing this deceptively simple, but eloquent, poem:

> 30 days hath *Tishre*, same as *Heshvan*, except the latter
>   sometimes has 29;
> *Kislev* also can have 29 or 30, whereas *Tevet* always has
>   29.
>
> *Shevat*, thanks God, has always 30, which doesn't help
> Because *Adar*
> Is totally confusing, both near and far.
>
> *Adar*, you see, has 29 days,
> But only during normal years.
> When a leap year, *Adar One* has 30,
> Moving many Jews to tears.
>
> *Adar Two*, that extra month which comes seven years
> Out of nineteen, that's clear,
> Has 29 days, which is quite regular
> And gives cause for lots of cheer.
>
> *Nisan*, always 30 days,
> *Iyyar*, always 29,
> *Sivan*, also 30 days,
> Which, to Jews, is always fine.
>
> *Tammuz?* 29 of course.
> *Av* is 30, just for show.
> *Elul* 29, and, with *mazel*,
> The Jewish calendar now you know!

The Worst Things a Jew Can Eat
Before the Yom Kippur Fast

The question has often arisen: what should a Jew eat before the long Yom Kippur fast? Traditionally, the feast is large and sumptuous, but constant vigilance has to be exercised, bearing in mind that the next drink of water is a long way away. So what should Jews *avoid* eating, immediately before "Kol Nidre" and the start of the Holy Day?

1   Pickled herring is frowned upon as a dessert.

2   Herring in sour cream is totally outlawed, since the meal has more than likely been *fleishig*.

3   Salted peanuts. Rabbi Zadok ben Akiba ruled that salted peanuts *were* acceptable just before "Kol Nidre" services, but since his father owned the largest peanut farm in Galicia, his ruling is usually ignored.

4   Pistachio nuts.

5   Potato chips of any variety, most especially barbecued.

6   Pizza with anchovies; see no. 2 above.

7   Straight anchovies on *challah*; see no. 1 above, and figure it out yourself. It's hard enough to be a Jew as it is, without adding to it.

The Most People in a Sukkah

Many have wondered why the Jews have not featured more prominently in the respected sport of telephone booth stuffing. But why bother with telephone booths, when you can challenge the *Sukkah*? Interestingly, the record for the most people crammed into a *Sukkah* is an old one and dates back to Eastern Europe where Jews had less to eat, and birth control was hard to come by, and "Be fruitful and multiply" was taken more literally than today.

> 278 people squeezed into the *Sukkah* of Avrum Abish Zylberberg of Dobromil, Poland, in 1904. (Actually it was part of Russia in 1901, part of Poland in 1903, part of Lithuania in 1910, part of Russia again in 1914, part of Poland again in 1916, and is now in the glorious Union of Soviet Socialist Republics.) When the 279th person, a third cousin twice removed ("and they can remove him again," said his aunt Bluma later), attempted to enter, the *Sukkah* flew apart so that it was no longer kosher for use during the holiday. Parts of the building landed as far away as Bilgoraj, a distance of twenty-seven Russian *versts*. "If my sister Yenta hadn't eaten so much," scowled Mr. Zylberberg later, "we could have made 300!"

The Classiest Sukkah

The *Sukkah* is by its very nature a temporary structure. Often having only three sides and a roof covered with leaves and branches, it is a most rickety building. Not so with the *Sukkah* of Ben and Victoria Hasselgrad in the backyard of their mansion in Marin County, California.

> The Hasselgrad *Sukkah* had wall-to-wall carpeting (actually Astroturf); grasscloth wallpaper and original paintings on each wall; a chandelier, hung precariously from the

cross-beam of the roof; and even a temporary (but flush) washroom, just off the side of the *Sukkah*.

"*Sukkos* is a gorgeous holiday," explained Victoria Hasselgrad, "so why not have a gorgeous *Sukkah*?"

"It was either this or a little place on the beach," added Ben Hasselgrad. "I figure, when you live on the beach, you never know when a giant wave might come and sweep our place away. At least in my own backyard, I *know* how long my *Sukkah* will last: I'm tearing it down next Wednesday."

The Shortest Time to Kosher a Stove for Passover

Even the least traditional Jew makes some effort to "kosher" the home for Pesach. Since this preparation involves ridding the home of all *chometz*, it is usually a long and tedious cleaning process. Not, however, for these award-winners.

1 Joe and Betty Sondheim, after five months' practice, managed to kosher their stove in time for Passover in April, 1987, in less time than twelve minutes using a Black and Decker acetylene torch. "It's an ugly job, but it had to be done," stated Mrs. Sondheim, pushing her welding glasses back from her eyes. "I've had it with Easy-Off. This [pointing to the torch] is my Easy-off!"

2 Harold and Roz Berman of Sydney, Nova Scotia, decided to kosher their home for Passover on April 3, 1973, by setting fire to it. "It wasn't an easy decision," laughed Harold from his detention cell in Sydney, where he was being held for arson. "But the house was hopeless. Crumbs in the living room, crumbs in the den; even crumbs in the beds. It would have taken us years to make it usable for Pesach. So Roz will spend this holiday at a kosher hotel in Miami Beach—I hear they're really nice—and I'm on a hunger strike until they provide me with matzah. At least in jail, there's not much bread around, you know. And concrete is much easier to clean than shag rugs. You should have seen it. Crumbs *everywhere*."

The Largest Etrog

The *etrog*, a citrus fruit used for ritual purposes during the Jewish holiday of Sukkot, is admired for its beauty, lemon-like size and odour, and peculiar shape.

The largest *etrog* was purchased by Harvey Fein of Massapequa, New York, for Sukkot in September, 1981. It weighted 32 lb. 4 oz., and was shaped like a watermelon. Mr. Fein constructed a large basket to carry it to and from synagogue, wowing his fellow congregants and giving himself a hernia.*

*Disregard the above "record." The authors of *The Unorthodox Book of Jewish Records & Lists* have just learnt that a hoax has been perpetrated. Fishl Tabachnick, the only fellow congregant of Harvey Fein who was *not* wowed by the size and shape of the record-breaking *etrog*, hired a private detective who discovered that the fruit was, in fact, a watermelon from Mr. Fein's own garden, painted yellow. "Only God can forgive him," declared Mr. Tabachnick, as we went to press. Moaned Fein: "All this because of a lousy, front-load mutual fund I urged Tabachnick to buy."

The Most Generous Afikoman Gift
Ever Recorded

Over the centuries, the ransom demanded by the child who "finds" the *Afikoman* has usually been a book or a few pennies. Inflation has been catching up, but even so the vision and ambition of some youngsters is breathtaking.

Brent Berenstain, the eight-year-old son of Dr. Harvey Berenstain of Houston, Texas, the prominent heart specialist, plastic surgeon, linguistic scholar, financier, and plumber, held out for the island of Antigua; April 16, 1978. In subsequent years, at the Passover *seder*, Brent demanded and got a private Lear jet to get to his island, and a fifty-foot yacht. He hopes to get an Atari for his Bar Mitzvah.

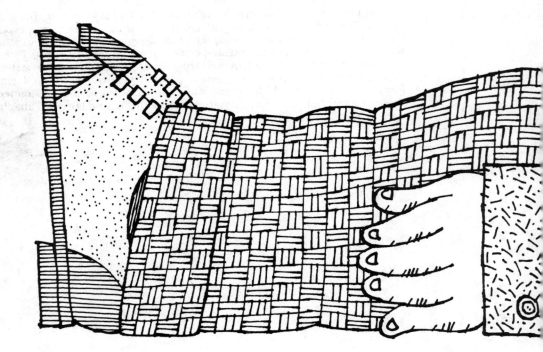

IX
The Jewish Family
(Plus Related Joys and Horrors)

The Most Popular Jewish Names for Children in the 1960s, 1970s and 1980s

For ages, Jewish parents have eagerly named their offspring after deceased parents and grandparents. But as a Jewish folksinger sang, "The times they are a-changin'."

Heather	Wendy	Conifer
Noel	Darcy	Korach
Shawn	Marcy	Amalek
Sean	Marci	Moab
Shaun	Marsee	Aphrodite
Shayne	Abdul	Scylla
Brendan	Wesley	Phedre
Kelly	Kevin	Calliope
Haley	Nevin	Leda
Halley	Ryan	Charybdis
Tracey	Hey, You	Eurydice
Stacey	Cory	Thor
Macey	Rory	Odin
Casey	Bradley	Jor-El
Raqui	Jennifer	Clark

The Jewish Life Cycle

1 Birth
2 *Nachas*
3 Circumcision/Naming
4 Baby bonds with grandparents
5 Baby bonds with parents
6 Dancing lessons
7 Shopping
8 Piano lessons
9 First credit card
10 First trip to orthodontist
11 First library card
12 Sleep-over camp
13 Bar/Bat Mitzvah
14 Rhinoplasty
15 First trip to the islands
16 First ten-speed bike
17 First psychoanalysis
18 First degree
19 Second degree
20 Third degree from mother on why not married yet
21 Marriage
22 Children (see 1–20, above)
23 Grandparenthood
24 *Nachas*
25 Death

The Most Successful Jewish Son to Go into His Father's Business

Jesus of Nazareth.

The Most Common Names of Jewish Girls in Haight-Ashbury in the 1960s

The Jewish heart beats faster when it recalls the great Jewish towns of history: Jerusalem; Seville, Spain; Warsaw, Poland; Haight-Ashbury, U.S.A. Jews lived in all of these places. Babies were born, and named.

1	Rainbow	7	April
2	Eden	8	May
3	Paradisa	9	Drizzle
4	Aurora	10	Summerfallwinterspring
5	Dawn	11	Borealis
6	Dusk		

The Most Popular Jewish Name Changes

Although inquisitions have not made the Jews change their faith, it has taken very little for Jews to change their names.

1   Ginsburg to Gaines.
2   Rabinowitz to Robbins.
3   Schoenberg to Belmont.
4   Goldstein to Christianson (when you really want to hurt Mom).
5   Yoshe Ber to Youngblood.
6   Nussbaum to Ness.
7   Rosenthal to Thall.
8   Gold to Copper.
9   Mowshovitz to Smith.
10 Pisher to La Fontaine.
11 Kinderlehrer to Cash.
12 Schneider to Taylor.
13 Rosenbaum to Roosevelt.
14 Eisen to Eisenhower.
15 Kanetsky to Kennedy.
16 Josephson to Johnson.
17 Nikitivitch to Nixon back to Nikitivitch.
18 Fendel to Ford.
19 Korenberg to Carter.
20 Razinsky to Reagan to Razinsky.

The Most Popular Names for Jewish Girls in the Southern United States

While the Jews have often been called a "race"—and for a while there, it looked like they were losing it—it is clear to any dispassionate observer that the Jews are more a people, a religion, a culture, a nation. The Jews who lived and still live in Ethiopia are black; the Jews of India look like the Indians amongst whom they have lived for centuries. Therefore, it is not surprising that Jews who have lived below the Mason-Dixon line in the United States should have picked up certain traditions from the natives around them. But why these?

1   Faygie Sue
2   Shayndel Mae
3   Shprintze Ellen
4   Hodel Lou
5   Yentel Fay
6   Roberta E. Leah
7   Jefferson Davida

The Most Macho Names Given to Jewish Male Children

While the Jewish faith has its sexist aspects, the people pride themselves on how few are dominant. Yet the attractions of macho language are undeniable, especially when Jewish children are born during the football season.

1   Bronco
2   Bonzo
3   Gonzo
4   Kyle
5   Bubba

The Most Popular Heroes of Jewish Kids

"Unhappy is the land that has no hero," complains a friend of the scientist Galileo in a Bertolt Brecht play. "Unhappy is the land that *needs* a hero," Galileo replies. Well, Jews need heroes. And a lot can be told from the heroes that Jewish children have.

Jewish Kids' Heroes in the 1930s

1 Albert Einstein
2 Stephen Wise
3 Edward G. Robinson
4 Their rabbi

Jewish Kids' Heroes in the 1980s

1 Reggie Jackson
2 Brooke Shields
3 Robin Williams
4 Wayne Gretzky
5 Michael Jackson
6 Pete Rose
7 Danny Rose, the only Jew on the list. Danny Rose is the kid in Grade 4 at the Moishe Kapoyra Hebrew School in Edmonton, Alberta, who came to school with chicken pox and infected everyone, forcing the institution to close down for three weeks in the fall of 1981.

The Smartest Jewish Grandchild

Jews have always tended to put great importance on brains, possibly because a good mind is something you can pack quickly when you've got to leave a country on short notice. For whatever reasons, the intelligence of grandchildren is prized above all. Which leads us to the obvious question: *Who* is the smartest Jewish grandchild?

1   Harold Weinstock of St. Catharines, Ontario, grandson of Earl and Anne Grossinger of Teaneck, recited the Four Questions of the Passover Service at birth; April 22, 1989.

2   Merwin Goldbaum of Newport, Rhode Island, performed his own ritual circumcision on the eighth day following his birth, on November 8, 1957, correctly predicting his future calling as a surgeon. (Submitted by his astonished, but no less proud, grandparents Daisy and Tom Goldbaum.)

3   Sharron Firestone of Rochester, New York, at the age of five weeks folded down the proper tab purchasing Israeli Bonds at a Yom Kippur service; wept through "Kol Nidre"; and, immediately following the holy day, began her own petition to fire the rabbi.

The Most "Kvelling" Jewish Grandparents

Jewish grandparents have good reason to be proud. Their grandchildren are beautiful, handsome, bright, intelligent, future-doctors, right? But sometimes grandparents have even more than usual cause to *kvell*.

Dr. and Mrs. Isadore Englander, whose daughter Priscilla has been President of the Zero Population Growth Association of Montreal, Quebec, for the past dozen years. On June 20, 1978, Priscilla Englander-Hoffman gave birth to an 8 lb. 4 oz. son, who emerged clutching an IUD in his gorgeous little hands.

The Rottenest Child of the Nicest Jewish Parent

When you plant asparagus, you tend to get asparagus. That's called biology. But as for Jewish children . . .

Christina Kowalski, *née* Chava Bernbaum of Chicago, the only daughter of Shaynde Bernbaum, the National President of the Women's League for Living Judaism, has not only joined the Moonies, Hare Krishna, and Jews for Jesus, but has also written two bestselling pamphlets on Scientology.

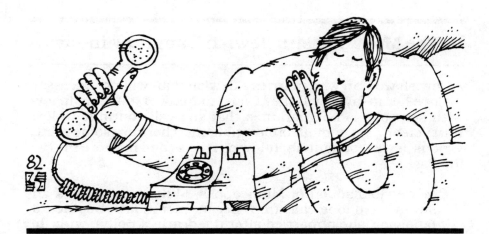

The Greatest One-liner Guilt Trips Laid upon a Jewish Child by a Jewish Mother

Yes, yes, we know. It's unfair, harsh, unkind, and just plain not nice to say that Jewish mothers cause guilt. Now that we've made that disclaimer, here they are:

1   "You never call."

2   "I'm sick. What do you care?"

3   "If the Nobel Committee in Sweden knew what sort of son you really are, they never would have nominated you for the Peace Prize."

4   "No, no, I'm sure that your graduate students in science are *far* more important than the woman who carried you inside her womb for nine months and went through a long, painful delivery."

5   "I find it hard to believe that your children don't know that they have a grandmother who lives only fifteen minutes away by car."

6   "You realize, of course, that if *I* spent as little time with *you* when you were a child, as *you* spend with me *now*, I would have been arrested."

The Most Spiteful Jewish Daughter-in-law

A Jewish woman who marries a Jewish man will not necessarily love her in-laws, will she? Come to think of it, falling in love with someone is no guarantee that she will continue to love *that* person. But enough philosophizing. There are some pretty vicious Jewish daughters-in-law out there, and here are the two finalists:

Merle Goldfadden of Minneapolis, Minnesota, always answers the phone calls from her mother-in-law, Sophie Rabinowicz (she remarried after the death of Solly), with the declaration, "You must have the wrong number."

Lucy Zoltak of Salt Lake City, Utah, whenever she runs into her mother-in-law on the street, bursts into Robert de Niro's famous speech from *Taxi Driver*: "You talkin' to *me*??? Are *you* talkin' to *me*?????" and whips out a toy gun.

The Jewish Child Who Stayed Home the Longest

It's not that Jewish parents are over-protective, or that their kids are demure or immature. You have to admit, it's a jungle out there.

1   Morris Slotnick of Linz, Austria, lived with his parents from the day of his birth, January 8, 1903, until 1935, when they emigrated to Sweden. He continued to live with them until one night in 1958, when his parents suddenly moved to Halifax, Nova Scotia, while little Morris—barely fifty-five—was sleeping.

"I just thought it was time for Morrie to be on his own," his father was quoted as saying in 1961. "There was no other way."

"It was too soon," Rachel Slotnick added, sobbing. "He's just a kid. I think we should go back. How will he manage? My grandfather Maury, rest in peace, whom Morrie is named after, didn't leave *his* parents' home until he was *sixty*."

2   Maury Weinstock of Danzig, Poland, did not leave his parents' home until his sixtieth birthday, in 1877, when his mother and father secretly moved to Linz, Austria. "It's true, it *was* his birthday," his father said later. "So let's just say that the move was a gift to *us*."

"I still think it was too soon," noted Rivka Weinstock, his mother.

The Most Rebellious Jewish Child

Ever since Joseph and his brothers, and probably earlier, Jewish children have tended to rebel against their parents and their faith. Although common to most youth, this rebelliousness is especially problematic for the Jews, who are not yet as numerous as the stars in heaven and the sand on the beaches, according to demographers.

Marty (after his great-grandfather, Mordecai) Bennett (away from his grandfather Benetinsky) ran off soon after his Bar Mitzvah to become a Zen Buddhist. After a number of years, he became a Sufi Muslim and joined an *ashram*. Just a few months later, he was attracted to Jews for Jesus, and then moved on to become a follower of Reverend Sun Moon. Losing interest, he fell in love with a Hare Krishna woman, and joined that group; but when he discovered that sex was frowned upon, he went to Israel, which moved his long-suffering parents to ecstasy. However, he joined Bahá'í, whose world headquarters is in Haifa. Shortly thereafter he befriended some Hassidim, and began to study at a *Yeshiva* in Jerusalem. At this point, his parents had him kidnapped and de-programmed back in the States. Said Mrs. Bennett: "I didn't raise *my* son to be a rabbi."

The Most Sexist Jewish Birth Announcements

Rabbi Chaim Silberschein, of the Silberscheiner sect of Hassidim from Silberschein, Poland, is recorded as publishing the following birth announcements in the *Silberscheiner Gazette*:

Rabbi Chaim Silberschein and his wife Gittel are pleased to announce the birth of their first child, a daughter, Hodel Zissl, on March 3, 1891.

Rabbi Chaim Silberschein and his wife Gittel announce the birth of their second daughter, Sheindl Reizl, a sister for Hodel Zissl, born June 15, 1892.

Rabbi Chaim Silberschein and his wife Gittel acknowledge the birth of their third daughter, Tzippa Nechama, a sister for Hodel Zissl and Sheindl Reizl, born May 26, 1893.

Rabbi Chaim Silberschein and his wife Gittel find it necessary to inform their friends that they have a fourth daughter, Tirzah Yocheved, another sister for Hodel Zissl, Sheindl Reizl, and Tzippa Nechama, born August 1, 1894.

Rabbi Chaim Silberschein and his new wife Hadassah have to announce the birth of their first child, a daughter, Devorah Malka, a half-sister for Hodel Zissl, Sheindl Reizl, Tzippa Nechama, and Tirzah Yocheved; January 20, 1898.

Rabbi Chaim Silberschein and his wife Hadassah are crushed to report the birth of their second daughter, Rivka Zipporah, a sister for Devorah Malka, and another half-sister for Hodel Zissl, Sheindl Reizl, Tzippa Nechama, and Tirzah Yocheved; December 8, 1901.

Rabbi Chaim Silberschein and his new wife Batsheva are devastated to announce the birth of their first child, Dinah Simma, and a half-sister for Rivka Zipporah, Devorah Malka, Hodel Zissl, Sheindl Reizl, Tzippa Nechama, and Tirzah Yocheved; February 27, 1905.

On the third day of Hanukkah, 1905, the revered Rabbi Silberschein either fell, or threw himself, under the baby carriage of his youngest daughter, and was tragically killed.

The Longest Time a Bubbe Not Visited

We know, we know, we know. If it weren't for *her*, our fathers would never have been born. And if it weren't for our fathers . . . Look, we've heard it all before. But what you probably *haven't* heard before is who holds the record for the longest time a *bubbe* was not visited:

> Mrs. Faigel Sheindel Fishlowitz of Bialystok, Poland, lived to be 118, which is not bad, for Poland. From the age of 72 until her death, she was not visited by even *one* of her 5 children, 23 grandchildren, 46 great-grandchildren, and 199 great-great-grandchildren. In the last few years of her life, Mrs. Fishlowitz *was* visited, however, by Brian Heatherton, an Anglican sociologist from England who happened to ask her the directions to the Bialystok train station. When Mrs. Fishlowitz finally released him, Heatherton knew the names of every one of the old woman's descendants, their bad habits, and the curses wished upon them daily for not visiting her.

People with Whom Jews May Not Have Sexual Relations

The Five Books of Moses are just bursting with people and things which Jews may *not* have sex with: sisters, brothers, sheep, and others you probably would not have thought of in a million years. Well, God did. But recent years have led to the demand for *more* people to be added to the "No No" list—to use the rabbinic term.

1   A woman fresh from the hairdresser.

2   A man fresh from the hairdresser.

3   A man without a Ph.D.

4   Anyone, the night before the United Jewish Appeal Walka-thon.

X
Food
(Nourishment, Noshes, Nibbles, Fressing and Other Jewish Obsessions)

80's Food Fad:
Pac-Matzah
Ball Soup
(Chicago, Illinois)

Classic Jewish Foods and Their Christian Counterparts

Hath not a Jew teeth? Taste buds? Salivary glands? So does the Christian. But they *do* work differently.

Jewish Food	Christian Food
mushroom soup	cream of celery soup
margarine	butter
sour pickles	sweet pickles
rye bread	white bread (how do they eat it?)
carrots	squash
salami	bologna
canned mushrooms	fresh mushrooms
mustard	relish
sweet and sour sauce	honey garlic sauce
cucumber	raw cauliflower*
lox and eggs	Eggs Benedict
boiled beef	Chateaubriand
bagels and cream cheese	flapjacks and syrup
tea with sugar held between the teeth	tea with granulated sugar from a spoon
seltzer water	Pepsi

*Note: Cauliflower, if cooked over two full hours, is Jewish.

123

Kosher Wines, According to Sweetness

You think your children are sweet? Read on.

1   Manischewitz Double Heavy Malaga (1948–82), sugar content 103%.*

2   Kedem Semi-heavy Malaga (1977), sugar content 94%.

3   Carmel Demi-sec Chateau Rabinowicz (any year), sugar content 55%.

4   Feinbaum's Extraordinarily Heavy Ultra Sweet Red, Extremely Undry (1988), sugar content unmeasurable.**

*A control double-blind study at Einstein Medical School in New York demonstrated that one sip of this wine causes immediate irreversible coma in diabetic laboratory rats.

**Feinbaum's Extraordinarily Heavy Ultra Sweet Red may be used as ketchup, as well as for ritual purposes.

The Most Jews Ever Seen in a
Chinese Restaurant

Over 240 (including 58 standing) at Yung Chow's, Pittsburgh, Pennsylvania, July 9, 1966.

388 at Lew Wing's for Irving Farfel's Bar Mitzvah party, Baltimore, Maryland, March 4, 1981.

The Most Chinese Ever Seen in a
Jewish Restaurant

19 at Hershel's Deli, Brooklyn, New York, October 28, 1974. All of them were visiting dignitaries from the People's Republic of China. (One of them was quoted afterwards as saying: "The trouble with Jewish food is, just forty-eight hours later, you're hungry again.")

The Earliest Known Jewish Graces after Meals

The "Birkat Ha-mazon" is an old and much revered blessing, recited by dozens of Jews, right around the world, after every meal. But what of the earliest known Jewish blessings given after meals? Ask no more!

1　*The Gutenberg Grace*, created by the Jews of Gutenberg, Germany, in the 1600s, was forceful, passionate, and brief:

> Hubba hubba hubba,
> Thanks for the grubba!
> Yeeaaaaaaaaaaaaahhhhhhhhhhh, GOD!!!

2　*The Bennington Birkat*, written in Bennington, Vermont, by Rabbi Jonas Wechsberg, is renowned for its poetry. Traced back to the early 1700s, it goes like this:

> Bless you for the bread,
> Bless you for the meat!
> But I bless you not at all
> For stewed carrots I won't eat!

> Bless you for the soup,
> Bless you for the fruit!
> But for over-cooked green beans
> I must remain mute!

3　The extremely ancient chant, really a cheer, of the Turkish Jews of the fifth century is still fresh and exciting:

> Give me a G! (The congregants respond "G!")
> Give me an O! (The congregants respond "O!")
> Give me a D! (The congregants respond "D!")
> Whaddayagot? (The congregants respond "GOD!")
> Whatdidhe*give* us?? (All scream out: "FOOOOOOOD!")

Since many of the Jews of Turkey starved to death in the sixth century, this last prayer has since been discredited.

The Most Elaborate Bar/Bat Mitzvah Foods

Jews have traditionally enjoyed throwing classy parties for their children's Bar/Bat Mitzvahs. So what's wrong with some classy catering as well?

1   A seven-stick *menorah* constructed entirely out of carrot and celery stalks, served at the Bar Mitzvah of Glenn Starkmann of Toronto, Ontario, 1955.

2   A huge *mezuzah* made out of potato salad; a mammoth Torah scroll made out of cole slaw; and a gigantic *tallis* made out of Nova Scotia lox, served at the Bat Mitzvah of Balfoura Zukerman of Chicago, Illinois, 1973.

3   A scale model (1 inch equals 5 feet) of the Holy Temple of Jerusalem sculpted out of chopped liver, at the Bar Mitzvah of Bernard Fidelman, Washington, D.C., 1979. Bernie's Bar Mitzvah occurred during the week of Tisha B'Av, the Jewish fast day that commemorates the destruction of the Holy Temple. As Bernie's father chewed reflectively on the Holy of Holies (on a Tam-Tam), he commented, "We felt we wanted Bernie to have a sense of the meaning of Jewish history."

The Longest Period of Time Any Jew Has Waited for a Corned Beef Sandwich

Although there have been dozens of cases of Jews waiting patiently to be served in a restaurant, none has been more extraordinary than that of Mrs. Ethel Hertzberg of Hollywood, Florida, on May 4, 1968.

At approximately 12:15 P.M. on that date, Mrs. Hertzberg entered Moishe's Deli to escape the rage of her husband, Alex, who still had not forgiven her for mocking his mother, Florrie, at his nephew Brian's Bar Mitzvah the previous Saturday. (Hope you have that all straight.)

At 12:35, Mrs. Hertzberg ordered a corned beef sandwich and a glass of tea. At 12:55, still not served, she asked for a side order of cole slaw, which she promptly received. At 1:22, she asked for some potato salad, which she also quickly received, but still no corned beef sandwich.

At 1:40, Mrs. Hertzberg ordered a chicken soup with kreplach, a chef's salad, and an order of blintzes, which she also soon received. At 2:11, she ordered some potato pancakes, a main order of chopped liver, a Coke, and a cheese cake.

At 2:51, exactly 2 hours and 16 minutes(!) after she had ordered her corned beef sandwich, Mrs. Hertzberg received it, with a hot glass of tea. The woman requested that it be wrapped so that she could take it home for her husband, Alex—who, unbeknownst to her, was packing his bags to return to their New York apartment.

(The owner of the restaurant, Moe Ganz, admitted later that the "late corned beef sandwich" is a trick of the trade to get customers to order while waiting. Mrs. Hertzberg's final bill was $37.45, which is not bad when she only wanted a corned beef sandwich and a glass of tea. During her marathon wait for the corned beef sandwich, Mrs. Hertzberg had broken not only her diet, but also seventeen of the dietary laws.)

The Largest Challah Ever Baked

The Grynstock Challah of Lodz, Poland, has become legendary. Put together by the students of the Grynstock Yeshiva for a Sabbath celebration on May 28, 1931, it took over a week to prepare and consisted of:

    400 cups oil
    3,200 teaspoons salt
    800 cups boiling water
    400 cups cold water
    1,600 packages dry yeast
    2,400 eggs
    5,600 cups flour
    12 pounds poppy seeds

The challah was baked in a giant oven, which was specially built for the occasion, at 475 degrees for 20 hours.

The Largest Challah Ever Burnt to a Crisp

The Grynstock Challah, of Lodz, Poland, baked by the Grynstock Yeshiva students in May, 1931. It should have been baked at 375 degrees, for 15 hours.

Great Jewish Diets

The Stillman, the Tarnower (rest in peace), the Beverly Hills (Judy Mazel, naturally)—Jews have been in the forefront of the dietary movements of the world since the Lord suggested that pig and shellfish might easily be dropped from shopping lists, nearly four thousand years ago.

1   *The Dig Your Grave with a Fork and See If I Care Diet*, written by Arnold Spite, was published in early 1982 by Radom House. It is now being remaindered across North America for 49¢, suggesting the importance of a good title.

2   *The Don't Visit Your Mother on Friday Nights Diet*, by Hana Grafshtein, published by S.S. Mynkind, Inc. This bestselling diet of 1974, which sold over 5 million copies in hard cover, urged Americans to "stay home and starve" rather than "visit Ma and gorge." The diet never caught on with traditional Jews, after the Lubavitcher Rebbe ruled that "honouring your father and mother takes precedence over keeping your figure."

3   *The Phoenix Diet*, by Rose Warson. See page 71.

131

The Largest Matzah Ball in History

The largest matzah ball ever made was created in Radom, Poland, on March 30, 1930, from ingredients donated by the Jews of Hamilton, Ontario.

The giant matzah ball was made by separating 250 dozen eggs, beating the yolks until they were frothy, beating the whites until they were stiff, adding 500 teaspoons salt, then adding 1,000 cups of matzah meal very slowly to the egg mixture.

The chilling of the giant matzah ball posed no difficulties: for 8 months a year in Radom, it is bitterly cold. The problem facing the hungry Jews of Radom was twofold: how does one find a kettle large enough to contain such a giant matzah ball, and how does one bring such a kettle of water to a boil?

The solution was suggested by Reb Imanuel Lefrak of Ostropol, who recommended the heating of the town *mikvah*. This was accomplished by setting fire to the bath-house. The giant matzah ball was catapulted into the midst of the flames, where it cooked rapidly, to the point of being a bit over-done.

The giant matzah ball, over twenty-two feet in diameter, fed the townspeople for three weeks. It was only after the feasting was over that someone pointed out that they should have made chicken soup in the *mikvah before* they set fire to the bath-house, to add some taste to the giant matzah ball. (Not that the cooking of a giant matzah ball in a giant, burning bath-house shows much taste in the first place.)

The Sharpest Horseradish Ever Served with Gefilte Fish

Gefilte fish and horseradish go together like love and divorce, milk and garlic, Israel and Syria. And speaking of *sharp* horseradish . . .

The horseradish made by Marilyn Lichtenstein of Hayward, California, was compared to kerosene and Mexican chili by her (late) husband Yankel, who died twenty-four hours after eating it; April 8, 1979. Mrs. Lichtenstein was acquitted by a jury of her peers, who found her gefilte fish delicious and requested the recipe.

The "EXXXXTRA HOTTT" horseradish manufactured by F. Strulovich and Sons was perfected on February 4, 1916. The family stopped manufacturing the horseradish on February 5, 1916, when they discovered that it ate through the glass containers and burned holes in their packing boxes. The horseradish recipe was confiscated by the United States government, and some historians of the Great War have suggested that the Strulovich family should be given credit for helping to bring that conflict to an early end. However, since the U.S. has consistently denied using chemical warfare, this cannot be verified.

The Driest Jewish Boiled Chicken Recipe

Let's get rid of some stupid myths. First, not all Jews are successful in business. Second, not all Jews are in show business. Third, not all Jews can cook well.

Take one chicken, previously frozen for more than two years but less than five. Place in a pot with one cup of distilled water. Set pot on electric stove over high heat, and leave for a weekend at the cottage. (Submitted by Golda Chertoff, San Diego, California; August 17, 1988.)

The Largest Piece of Matzah

Matzah—a little taste of sawdust on earth, according to some; a lovely change from bread, in the opinion of others. But a must on Passover, to most. Matzah is usually the size of a large paperback—and just as edible. But what of the largest piece in history?

The largest piece of matzah was baked in Riga, Latvia, on April 18, 1901. It was over 50 feet long and 80 feet wide and was baked ritually by Rabbi Berl Levinsky. Rather than being used in the Passover *Seder*, however, the giant matzah was climbed on by the Rabbi and his wife and eleven children, who used it to float to safety and, ultimately, to America. They arrived in the New World three months and six days after they had left Eastern Europe, having survived by eating over half of their "raft."

The Greasiest Latke

The record for the greasiest latkes must be held by Debby Abramowitz of Tucson, Arizona. They have been known to slide off the plate of the prospective eater, the fork of the prospective eater, and even the tongue of the prospective eater, December 1983, 1984, 1985, 1986, 1987, 1988.

"I misread the recipe on the side of the package," admits Ms. Abramowitz. "Where it said one *cup* oil, I used one *gallon*, and the family loved it, so I continue to cook them that way."

"It's *fun* to try to catch the latkes as they slide around the table," declares her youngest son, Lance.

The Saltiest Lox

The reason why lox is so important in the diet of the Jewish people is still unknown. Nowhere in the Bible or Talmud is it mentioned; none of the great rabbis comment upon its worth. Nevertheless, Jews can't get enough of it. (Not surprising, either, at $27.50 a pound.)

The saltiest lox in history is, without doubt, the lox eaten by the furrier Levi Rosenbloom of Busk, Poland, on July 17, 1893, on the occasion of his son Yossi's circumcision.

Tense and excited (the *mohel* had been seen drunk earlier that morning), Rosenbloom dived into the lox that had been laid out for the reception. After eating only five pieces of the smoked salmon, the furrier clutched at his throat, leapt through the window of his home (it was closed at the time; in Busk, Poland, even July is cold) directly into Busk Lake, and drank upwards of ten gallons without stopping.

When later interviewed in his office, Mr. Rosenbloom was quoted as saying: "If *that* was lox, it must have had a long love-affair with a school of anchovies before it was smoked."

The Most Versatile Jewish Food

When one thinks of Jewish foods, one thinks of blintzes, latkes, corned beef, and so on. But as far as *versatility* in Jewish food is concerned, most scholars agree that the bagel stands supreme. According to records at the Hebrew University in Jerusalem, bagels have been used for:

- holding up a table during a meal in a *Sukkah*.
- placing the handles of the holy Torah scrolls in, to steady the precious object in the Ark.
- a skullcap, when no other was available.
- a wedding ring, when the best man at the wedding of Larry Cornblum, of Toronto, forgot to bring one for the bride.
- felling the mighty Goliath, as reported in the Book of Samuel. "Had it been a *fresh* bagel that the young David threw at the giant Philistine, instead of a stale one," notes Yaacov Lupkofsky of Bar Ilan University in Israel, "Jewish history might have turned out quite differently."

The Most Carp in a Single Jewish Bathtub

For centuries, East European Jews have kept carp in their bathtubs (when they had them), alive and fresh until the giant fish were needed for making gefilte fish for the holiday.

The record for the most carp in a single bathtub was achieved by Bluma Rubenstein of Baltimore, Maryland, on September 1, 1953. The number was recorded and verified by a marine biologist at the Baltimore Aquarium—114.

"I kept getting more and more letters, telling me of cousins and aunts and uncles who were coming in to Baltimore for that year's Rosh Hashana," declared Mrs. Rubenstein. "So I just kept buying more and more carp to make my justifiably famous gefilte fish."

A few days later Mrs. Rubenstein discovered that all the letters were part of a hoax perpetrated by a no-good son-in-law, Harvey Dubrov (since divorced by Mrs. Rubenstein's older daughter, Basya). In the interim, unfortunately, her husband Irv absent-mindedly stepped into the tub while using an electric shaver. Over forty of the fish were cooked, along with Mr. Rubenstein, leading to a very sad High Holiday season for the family, indeed, although the gefilte fish served by Bluma after the funeral were as good as ever.

The Most Ecumenical Jewish Dishes

An "ecumaniac" has been defined as someone who thinks that every religion is superior to his own. Well, Jews are second to none when it comes to longing for ecumenism. This democratic and loving ideal derives from an ages-long desire to remain alive. The following list of Ecumenical Jewish Dishes (originally gleaned from the classic, *The Goy of Cooking*) may well help to make Judaism more palatable to Christians, and vice versa.

1 Bacon and lox.
2 Spanish-Portuguese omelette.
3 Boiled Chicken-à-la-King.
4 Tsimmes and Mussels (alive alive-O).
5 Crablach.
6 Ham-en-tashen.
7 Candied latkes.
8 Cream of chicken soup.
9 Lobster in sour cream.
10 Herring chowder.

XI
Jews in Suburbia
(and Other Chosen Ghettos)

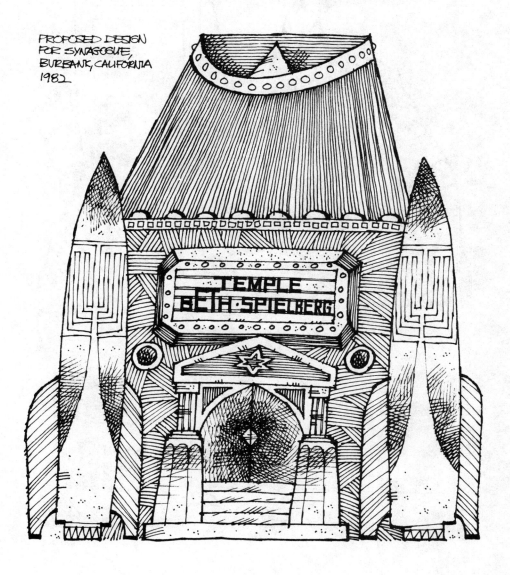

PROPOSED DESIGN
FOR SYNAGOGUE,
BURBANK, CALIFORNIA
1982

The Most Exclusive Jewish Country Club

Jewish country clubs have been in existence since the first Jew was denied entrance to *another* country club. These impressive gathering places are sprinkled across North America—the Westwood in St. Louis, the Lake Shore Club in Chicago, the Hillcrest Country Club in Los Angeles, the Columbian Club in Dallas.

The *most exclusive* Jewish country club was founded near Langley, Virginia, by Asher Frankel in 1928, in response to his being kept out of a Christian club. As of the fall of 1988, this most exlusive of all Jewish country clubs, the Roosevelt, was being run by Arthur Franklin, grandson of the founder. Mr. Franklin will not allow any Jew to join.

Said the owner, now a Unitarian: "You know, if you let just *one* Jew in, they start to take over. It almost happened to my grandfather."

The Most Needless Examples of
Wall-to-Wall Carpeting

Wilma and George Gilbert of Oshawa, Ontario, had wall-to-wall carpets installed in their bungalow, including the bathroom, up the walls, and even on the ceiling.

"I know it seems foolish," protested Mrs. Gilbert, "but when you're raised with certain values, you've got to be true to them. Carpets *are* important, you know. You can get splinters from wood, and my feet tend to get cold on anything else but rug. And it was a *great* deal."

Noah and Ruth Friedhoff of Cincinnati, Ohio, went so much into debt putting wall-to-wall carpeting throughout their four-bedroom home that they were unable to meet their mortgage payments, and lost the house; November 1, 1965. The Friedhoffs moved into a three-bedroom apartment, where they promptly put in wall-to-wall carpets on every floor, even on the underground garage, leading to their eviction; January 14, 1966. By the fall of 1966, the couple were on welfare. On December 23, 1966, Mr. Friedhoff was arrested while breaking into a broadloom factory. When Mrs. Friedhoff visited her husband in jail, she was caught laying a carpet in his cell, and was arrested as well.

"Some Jews wear skullcaps; others visit Israel," the Friedhoffs stated in court, in early 1967. "*We* believe in carpets. I thought this country allowed for freedom of religion."

The Best Greetings to Jewish Nose-job Patients

One of the major Jewish problems—well, certainly a perennial one—has been how to greet, or what to *say* to, a Jewish friend who has undergone plastic surgery on his or her nose—a rhinoplasty, as the medical profession refers to it, not without a tinge of humour. After talking with dozens of surgeons (and we know it was dozens, we got billed by every one) and thousands of patients, the authors have collected the most suitable statements to make to Jews who have received "nose jobs."

1   "Well, well, well. I guess *now* you'll have to buy a bottle opener."

2   "Look at you! A thing of beauty and a *goy* forever."

3   "I realize that you always wanted to have it done. But Cyrano de Bergerac coped very well without a nose job, you know."

4   "I'll miss all those balancing tricks you did with the tables and chairs in the high school lunchroom."

5   "It'll be exciting for you to finally be able to drink from a glass like normal people."

6   "It looks as though you've gone ahead and cut off your nose to spite your race."

The Most Luxurious Kosher Vacation Hideaway

The authors commissioned a survey of more than five thousand Jewish travel agents around the world:

1   Bernstein's of Aruba.
2   Weinstock's of Havana (nationalized in 1962 by Castro).
3   Katz of the Catskills.
4   Barry's of Birobijan (turned into Boris's by Stalin, 1938).
5   Marty's of Martinique.
6   Shlomo's of Sicily (where he'll offer you a deal on a room that you can't refuse).
7   Buddy's of Budapest (nationalized in 1951).
8   Pinchas's of Pinsk, later merged with Minna's of Minsk.

Jewish Cases of Spontaneous Combustion

The earliest known case of spontaneous combustion involving a Jewish person took place at the time of Moses, when a bush suddenly burst into flames while the future leader was tending his flock of sheep. Since the bush was not consumed, the fire was not reported to the authorities until years later, in the Bible. Usually, though, cases of spontaneous combustion are immediately reported to the authorities—the insurance company and the police—often before the fire has got a really good hold.

The most celebrated case of modern Jewish spontaneous combustion occurred on July 8, 1934, in Buffalo, New York, in the offices of Balfour Pritzker, Dry Goods. According to Pritzker, his body suddenly burst into flame. He rolled around on the rug, trying to put the fire out, but the flames caught the curtains and immediately spread throughout the four-storey factory. Pritzker leapt from his

second-storey window and was miraculously unhurt, there being a fortunately discarded mattress under his window, and the rush of air as he was falling extinguishing the flames before they had time to burn his body.

Officer Tom Robinson of the Buffalo Police Department marvelled at the "astonishing coincidence that this act of spontaneous combustion should happen only two weeks after Mrs. Pritzker took out a $2 million policy on Mr. Pritzker's place of business, and at the end of the worst year he ever suffered financially."

The court later agreed that there was combustion, but disagreed with Pritzker's lawyer on how spontaneous it was.

Strange Customs of Rare Jewish Communities and Sects

The tiny Jewish population of Polynesia, descendants of Jews who drifted there after the Destruction of the Temple nearly two thousand years ago, uses coconut shells as skullcaps and makes prayer shawls out of giant palm leaves. The wearing of grass skirts in synagogue is permitted by the Rabbi of Temple Palua Mani Mani (Reform), only.

The mountain Jews of Tibet, who came there after fleeing from Czarist Russia at the turn of this century, still pray for the health of the Czar, while throwing snow over their shoulders and spitting three times. Yak meat stew is a highly-prized Sabbath delicacy; the horns of the deceased animal are blown on the High Holidays to call the congregation to repentance.

The Jews of Guatemala, who migrated from Labrador in the 1920s, build giant "snow men" out of sand, wear galoshes in 90-degree weather, and say "Hag sameach, *eh*?" Reindeer stew is a highly-prized Sabbath delicacy, and the horns of the deceased animal are blown on the High Holidays to call the congregation to repentance. Papaya and guava juice are used for *Kiddish*.

The Jews of the United States build enormous, expensive synagogues and Temples, visit Israel regularly, think Dick Cavett is a genius, and tend to vote Democratic until they become extremely successful in business.

The Most Commonly Given Excuses for a Jewish Child to Miss Hebrew School

Hard as it may be to believe, not every Jewish child looks forward eagerly to going to Hebrew School. What, then, are the most common excuses given for skipping a day?

1   Tennis lesson
2   Braces coming off
3   Dancing lesson
4   Braces coming on
5   Sesame seed caught in braces
6   Dance recital
7   A long line-up at Colonel Sanders
8   Mom was too tired to drive
9   The car door stuck
10 Tennis play-offs
11 It was raining
12 It wasn't raining

The Synagogues That Held Out the Longest Before Being Forced to Move

In the United States over the past few generations, neighbourhoods have often "changed." Considerable numbers of congregants move away from their synagogues.

In 1978, Congregation B'nai Morris of Newark, New Jersey, finally moved from its downtown location. Since the shul was first built in 1911, the neighbourhood had changed from Jewish to white Protestant to black Protestant to Puerto Rican Catholic, to Cuban Catholic, to pagan, to anarchist. At the time of the congregation's move, the only person who still prayed there—early every morning—was an Italian cleaning lady.

On April 9, 1981, Temple Har Sinus of Detroit, Michigan, was sold to a Moslem mosque after the membership had dwindled from 800 families to 3. "We had *thought* of moving, back in 1946, when the neighbourhood first started to change, but we just couldn't get a good price," said the board president, Marv Fischer. "But I'm glad we held out. Sheik Farhadd gave us a cheque for $4 million, which should just be enough for a down-payment on a store-front in West Bloomfield Hills. Thank God for the oil crisis."

The Biggest Show-offs in Jewish Suburbia

Ever since the Breastplate of Aaron—and it *was* gorgeous—some Jews have been guilty of conspicuous consumption. But then the Jews never built Notre Dame or the Mosque of Omar, so they had to get their jollies *somewhere*.

1   Mrs. Maureen Rappoport of Great Neck, New York, salts her front walk each winter with Accent (MSG).

2   Rabbi Zacharia Teppleman of Paris, France, puts on La-Coste *tefillin* every morning, with a tiny alligator on the head and arm pieces.

3   Mrs. Babs Weissbrod of Toronto, Ontario, has an interior decorator who designs her *Sukkah* each year.

4   Aharon Kranzberg, a Hassid of the Rothschilder sect in Crown Heights, New York, wears a Gucci *shtreimel*.

5   Mel Fonzberg, a high-class "enforcer" for his "social club" in Chicago, has a black leather *tallis* with "God's Angels" emblazoned on the back in day-glo sequins, designed by Ringling Bros. of Sarasota, Florida.

XII
Occupations
(Doctors of the Mind and Body Plus Some Jews Who Couldn't Stand the Sight of Blood)

The Most Common Jewish Occupations of the Twentieth Century

Generalities are always risky. But then again, so is any book that purports to be humorous. Without further ado, Jew-Jobs:

1 Doctor
2 Lawyer
3 Accountant
4 Dentist
5 Tailor
6 Movie star
7 Writer
8 Company Second Vice-President
9 Insurance salesman
10 Nobel Prize winner
11 Nobel Prize nominee
12 Psychiatrist
13 Solo violinist
14 Furrier
15 Furrier turned solo violinist

Typical Salaries for Employees in Jewish Communal Work in Major North American Cities, 1989

1   The Executive Vice-President of the Federation of Jewish Charities: $85,000.
2   The Athletic Director of the Jewish Community Centre: $65,000.
3   The rabbi of a major Conservative synagogue: $78,000.
4   The rabbi of a major Orthodox shul: $10,800.
5   The rabbi of a major Reform temple: $99,000, with car.
6   A Hebrew School teacher of twenty years experience: $19,250.
7   The janitor at the Hebrew School: $33,000.

The Jewish Stress Scale

The Social Re-adjustment Scale has taken on great significance recently, as many doctors have come to believe that stress lies behind heart attacks and other major illnesses. Jews are particularly susceptible to stress under certain circumstances and, accordingly, should be aware of the dangers to their emotional and physical well-being created by the following situations:

1   Divorcing your spouse, and she gets the car.
2   Staying married to your spouse, but *he* drives the car.
3   Your son joining the army.
4   Your son joining a religious cult.
5   Your daughter starting her own religious cult.
6   Going to jail for what your partner did, the lousy *gonif.*
7   Going to jail for what *you* did, you stupid idiot.
8   Your daughter running off with a born-again gymnasium teacher at her high school.
9   Throwing a Bar Mitzvah for your son.

10 Throwing your son out of the house one week before his Bar Mitzvah, when all the invitations are out.
11 Being fired from your place of employment, when you *own* the place, for God's sake.
12 Your daughter choosing to go into Jewish education as a profession, which means you'll have to support her forever.
13 Your mother coming out and finally admitting that she always loved your sister Lucille better than you, despite all those years you actually did what she told you to do, when what she told you to do was destructive to your physical and emotional well-being.

Famous Jewish Law Firms

Louis Nizer, Marvin Mitchelson, Marvin Belli—the Jew and law go together like herring and sour cream. Okay, okay, so maybe Belli isn't Jewish; what are you going to do—sue?

1 Siman Tov and Mazel Tov, brothers-in-law
2 Chen, Chessed and Rachamim, Jerusalem, barristers and solicitors
3 Schvartz, Veiss, Braun, Roth and Blau, lawyers
4 Edel, Ehrlich, Ziess, Fein and Shayn, Inc.
5 Momzer, Zhlob & Kvetch, divorce lawyers
6 Chaim, Tovim, and Sholom
7 Cohen, Levi & Yisroel
8 Leopold and Loeb, criminal law

Famous Jewish Marksmen

Buffalo Bill Cody, Wild Bill Hickok, Annie Oakley—the list of great marksmen is long. Less long is the list of Famous Jewish Marksmen.

Chaim Bronowski of Plonsk, Poland, was considered the most astounding marksman of the nineteenth century. Fighting in over fifty-three battles with Russian and Finnish troops, he managed to pump more than 2,700 bullets into his left and right feet. Said Mr. Bronowski, in the Plonsk hospital after his fifty-third self-attack: "Of *course* I aim the gun downward when the enemy is attacking. You want I should *kill* someone?"

Duddl Davidowicz of Pinsk, Russia, was considered the most amazing marksman of the first quarter of the twentieth century. In over two dozen skirmishes and more than twenty major battles during the Great War (1914–1917 for Russia), Davidowicz shot down more than 947 birds. Said Davidowicz, in a Bolshevik prison in 1919: "Of *course* I aimed the gun upward when the enemy was attacking. Otherwise, I could have *killed* someone!"

Specifically Jewish Diseases

Dwarfs tend to be short; clumsy people tend to bump into things. Is it any wonder that a group such as the Jews should have its own disease tendencies?

1	Guilt	7	Asthma
2	Heartache	8	Heart disease
3	Diabetes	9	Allergy
4	Aggravation	10	Nail biting
5	Acne	11	Flat feet
6	Malocclusion		

Famous Jewish Mountain Climbers*

*Are you crazy? A man could get killed.

Props Neckme. 25·VI·82

The Most Jewish Doctors

The record for the most Jewish doctors per square inch was set in Tel Aviv, Israel, in 1962. During that year, the number of doctors numbered 450 for every 1,000 residents. This led to extreme distress and unemployment among the medical men, until a number of them decided to take law degrees at the Hebrew University, then went into malpractice specialties.

Said the first to graduate, Yakov Gruenberg, later one of the first millionaires in the Jewish State: "It's a joy. No house calls, my own hours, and I end up with all the money I *would* have made as a doctor, and more. Come to think of it, it's the exact *same* money I would have made as a doctor, since it goes from the patients to the guilty doctor to me, eventually."

The Fewest Jewish Doctors

The fewest Jewish doctors per 1,000 people was in Damascus, Syria, 1981, when there was absolutely *no* medical man or woman of the Jewish faith for over 3 million people.

"It's a shame, really," commented Dr. Moshe Shahn, the last Jewish doctor to leave Syria, in 1977. "With not a single rotten malpractice lawyer in the entire country, I had half a mind to stay."

The Most Overwhelming Act of Bikur Cholim

Mrs. Rhoda Liptzin of Reno, Nevada, would visit every sick person at Mt. Kilimanjaro Hospital of Reno at least twice a day, from January 1, 1948, until her death.

During her nearly five years of non-stop visiting the sick, Mrs. Liptzin carried more diseases from room to room than a swarm of bees carries pollen. Patients with bad cases of the flu caught hepatitis; patients with pneumonia picked up herpes (Mrs. Liptzin loved to kiss all the patients on the lips when she first entered a room); patients with broken legs were stricken with German measles; patients with chicken pox saw their sickness spread throughout the hospital daily. Even visitors to the hospital were felled by Liptzin's germs.

Before Mrs. Liptzin finally died, on March 28, 1953, she was talked into donating her body to science. "We are ecstatic she did," said Dr. Ross McNeil of the staff of epidemiology at Mt. Kilimanjaro Hospital. "She was a walking encyclopedia of diseases when she finally went. We don't even know what finally got her—it could have been one of a thousand germs. At least, that's all we've been able to label until now. Some students plan to study her through every year of medical school."

The Schmaltziest Jewish Violinist

Jews and violins go together like Kissinger and power. Everyone knows this, but no one before now has ever tracked down the Schmaltziest Jewish Violinist. We have.

The schmaltziest Jewish violinist in history was Yascha Adler of Rumania, Rumania (now part of Hungary), who lived there from 1868–1929, and played there from 1871–1929.

Adler was so schmaltzy that when he played his violin at the Moulin Rouge Café (now The People's Eatery) the patrons would weep, the owner would weep, the bartenders would weep, and horse-and-buggy drivers out in the street would cry so much that they could not see where they were going. A horse, Ferdele, also used to weep when Yascha Adler played, but this was later discovered to be an eye infection.

All this weeping, it should be noted, occurred when Adler played polkas and joyous music. When he played sad music, there was mass hysteria.

XIII
Inventors
(Breakthroughs and Breakdowns)

Jews Who Never "Made It"

In spite of what our friends say, and in spite of what our enemies say, Jews are not *all* successful. In fact, some do rather poorly. And some, like these, do *rotten*.

1   Jewish Dior, dress manufacturer, 7th Ave. and 35th St., Manhattan, 1933–1977, now Miami Beach, Florida.

2   Marvin Stone, inventor of the "Pet Stone," which he began to sell at his Marv's Variety in Grand Rapids, Michigan, three weeks after the Pet Rock craze began.

3   Hanukkah Coward, an unproduced songwriter and playwright, mal-vivant and wit(less) of Spokane, Washington.

4   Hans Jewish Anderson, a story-teller at the Newark Public Library.

5   Lawrence Cutratesky, manufacturer of Six-Up, a diet soft drink sold in non-returnable bottles with returnable cap.

6   Reuben Kubelovitch, creator of "Reuben's Cube," which has eight sides and sixteen possible combinations. Since seven of its sides are the same colour, it takes the average four-year-old less than five seconds to solve the puzzle; Reuben would take over three hours.

Inventions Jews Will Invent Before Long

The polio vaccine, of which we are very proud. The Wasserman test, of which we are proud. The atom bomb, which we would rather not talk about. But what is to come?

1. Lobsters *with* scales.

2. A cure for tennis elbow.

3. A portable, $4.95 machine to smoke your own salmon at home.

4. An answering machine that prevents people who call from hanging up until they leave their name and phone number.

5. An answering machine that screens out all calls from solicitors for the United Jewish Appeal or Israeli bonds.

6. A new calendar with no Monday.

Great Jewish Conversions

Most people consider the conversion of Saul on the road to Damascus (he changed his name to Paul to avoid hurting his mother) to be one of the great Jewish conversions. And, in fact, it *was* pretty good. But that, of course, was from Judaism to you-know-what. Jews have also been converted in other ways, at other times.

Stephen Schwartz of Passaic, New Jersey, was a secular Jew with pagan leanings until November 5, 1975, when he was playing football for his school, Daniel Ellsberg Senior High.

As he dropped back to pass (he was the quarterback, turn the evil eye), he saw a bright light and heard a loud, deep voice. He paused, in religious ecstasy, only to be tackled by three enormous men from the opposite team.

Schwartz's side lost the game 84–7, but the young Stephen, then 17, won his soul. He went off to a *Yeshiva* in Jerusalem, where he is still studying Talmud.

"I haven't lost a son; I've gained a fanatic," says his distraught mother, Mabel.

"Be thankful he was hit by only *three* other players," adds his father Harry. "If he'd been downed by five or six guys, he might be in Mecca now, studying Islam."

The Fastest Jew on Land

As can well be imagined, the number of qualifying Jews is great. To the best of our knowledge—and *we* work pretty quickly, we have to admit—this one holds the record:

> Vladimir Tumanov achieved the speed of 485 m.p.h. on October 9, 1964, from Leningrad.
>
> Since this speed was attained without the use of a motorized vehicle, and in bare feet, it is all the more remarkable.
>
> "Not really," protested Tumanov modestly, in Vienna the day after his astonishing run. "When your request to emigrate is turned down, when you are called a parasite, and when it looks like prison cooking for the next twenty years, you learn to run fast, *real fast.*"

Famous Mistakes in the World of Science

The marriage of Dr. Oscar Weisskopf, the Dean of Medical Research at Johns Hopkins University, to Nancy Fineblit of Miami on May 30, 1961. The former Miss Fineblit caused the brilliant Dr. Weisskopf nothing but heartache and woe while, if he had followed his heart, he would have married Tammy Semmelman, a witty and charming neighbour and a first cousin of the publisher of this book, who would have given him a proper and peaceful Jewish home so that he might have been free to cure heart disease, psoriasis, and God knows what else.

Zygmund "Sammy" Samuelson's formula explaining the essence of reality. A tinkerer and toy-maker working in a Russian patent office at the turn of the century, he was forced to leave his scientific notes behind when he escaped the Revolution. Upon his arrival in the U.S., he reconstructed most of his material from memory. His one mistake, $E = mc^3$, caused him to miss the Nobel Prize by just one number.

A List of Ancient Jewish Measurements and Their Recent Usage

The inch, the foot, the pound, the litre, the quart—measurements all. But few know of the original measurements from the Bible and Talmud, and their importance to the way we all see the world. The following is a list of measurements mentioned in the Torah and later Jewish texts, and how the Jews interpreted them:

The Cubit is the length from an adult Jew's knee, as he falls to his dirt floor in anger, to his elbow, as he leans against it on his orange-crate kitchen table.

The Zeret is the length from a thumb, outstretched to hitch a ride to the New World, to the tip of the baby finger, extended to catch a snowflake for nourishment.

The Kor is the amount of wheat gathered by a poor Jew from the field of a wealthy aristocrat in one hour.

The Kab is the amount of herring that can be eaten before partaking of a glass of water.

The Chelek is the length of time a Jew can listen to the insult of a stupid sermon before leaping up in anger and rage.

XIV
Jewish Records
and Lists
Which Didn't Fit into
Any Topic for Reasons
Too Numerous to List
(or we'd have to include another list)

The Most Countries One Jew Had to Leave

For reasons too absurd to mention, even for this book (we should give our enemies ideas?), Jews have occasionally found themselves *persona non grata* at various moments in their history. One such era was the fourteenth century, when the record was set for the most countries one Jew had to leave:

> Asher Fruchter, of Frankfurt, Germany, was asked to leave his native village at the age of nineteen, when he stooped to pick up a coin which the son of the mayor saw at about the same time; March 21, 1344.
>
> Fruchter moved to Paris, France, where he had barely found an apartment before he was asked to leave: the landlord's baby caught a cold that day, and there was no one new in the city except him to blame; April 22, 1344.
>
> Fruchter moved on to Brussels, Belgium, which he was promptly asked to leave; he arrived on a Sunday, and he should have been in church; April 28, 1344.
>
> Fruchter then tried Amsterdam, Madrid, Gibraltar, Casablanca, Cairo, Constantinople, Rome, Athens, London, and finally a small village in Peru, but each country in turn invited him to leave.
>
> Fruchter ended up in Buenos Aires on January 2, 1345, where he set up the most successful travel agency of the Middle Ages.

People Who Should Have Been Jewish, and Probably Are If They Go Back Far Enough

1 Albert Schweitzer
2 Dr. Tom Dooley
3 Eleanor Roosevelt
4 Shakespeare
5 Mother Teresa
6 Lech Walesa
7 Alan Alda

The Oldest Known Jewish Nursery Rhyme

While Jews can claim many firsts in history—the first case of diabetes, the first bridge player, the first heart attack—there are some firsts which are shrouded in the mists of ancient history. Gradually, however, the sands of time shift to reveal their secrets. A lucky find in the diggings at Ebla has gone far towards clearing up a long-standing folklore controversy. In loose translation, it goes like this:

Monday's child is pretty good looking;
Tuesday's child is gorgeous, turn the evil eye.
Wednesday's child should look both ways when crossing
    the road, he shouldn't get hurt, God forbid;
Thursday's child can always go into his father's business.
Friday's child is a sweetheart and a mensch,
Saturday's child caused his mother nothing but heartache
    for making her labour on Shabbas.
But the child that thinks Sunday is the sabbath day
    Will hurt his parents and go astray, the bum.

The Toughest Hassidim

In many neighbourhoods in the United States, religious members of Hassidic groups have found it necessary to protect themselves. The following were judged to be the toughest Hassidim in North America today, Canada included:

1   The Montrealer Hassidim traditionally drink out of *Yahrtzeit* glasses while they are still lit.

2   The Bostoner Hassidim wear bullet-proof prayer shawls.

3   The Ann Arborer Hassidim have mined streets in their neighbourhood to prevent cars from disturbing their Sabbath.

4   The Bronxer Rebbe's followers wear football helmets instead of the traditional fur *shtreimel*.

Little-known Jewish Superstitions

Getting caught in the middle of a pogrom is unlucky. This superstition originated in the late nineteenth century in Russia and various other countries in Eastern Europe, where getting caught in the middle of a pogrom was extremely unlucky.

*Black cats should **not** be avoided.* In 1844, Nissim Assad, of Morocco, was stranded in the middle of the desert for some ten days, following a nasty quarrel with a camel driver. A black cat crossed his path; he ate it, and the protein kept him alive until he was rescued two weeks later by a tribe of Bedouin, who were good ones.

If you spill salt, do not throw it over your shoulder in case a Cossack is standing behind you. This superstition, followed for over a century by Russian Jews, was proven invalid when Issachar Slomovitz of Pinsk (or was it Minsk?), upon spilling some salt, picked some up and threw it over his shoulder. It flew right into the eyes of a Cossack who was about to club Slomovitz on the head, temporarily blinding the brute and thereby allowing the Jew to escape to America, where his children and grandchildren are doing very well.

Jews Will Rogers Never Met
Or He Never Would Have Said: "I never met a man I didn't like"

1 Howard Cosell
2 Jerry Lewis
3 Ivan Boesky
4 Your Uncle Hymie

The Longest Period of Time Any Jew Ever Spoke Without Using His Hands to Gesture

As every Jew is aware, this ancient people tends to use its hands a great deal when speaking. So, for that matter, do Italians, Greeks, and Spaniards. So, too, do Moroccans. Come to think of it, so do Englishmen, Turks, and Germans. And Frenchmen. You know, Canadians and Mexicans do, too.

Well, anyway, the longest period of time a *Jew* has ever spoken without using his hands was 14 minutes and 9 seconds, on February 2, 1912, in the Ukraine, Russia.

The incredible record-breaker was named Yechiel Yitzchak Zurowell; the listener was Gershon Elimeilech Fiersztein; the exact location was outside the local synagogue; the time was after morning prayers. The temperature was 73 degrees below zero, Fahrenheit, which is nearly as cold in Celsius, and even Mr. Zurowell found it too cold to use his hands—at least for those astonishingly long 14 minutes.

However, at the 14:09 point in his record, the listener said something favourable about the Czar of Russia, at which point Zurowell, somewhat a radical, drew his hands out of his pockets and shook them in rage at Fiersztein.

Zurowell immediately got a severe case of frostbite on all ten fingers, which did not hurt half as much as the severe beating he received at the gloved hands of the Czarist Secret Police, who had witnessed Zurowell shake his fists at the Czar.

The Most Famous Scores in Religious Texts

1. Methuselah 969, Moses 120.
2. Samuel II, Kings I.
3. Chronicles II, Kings II.
4. Trinity 3, God 1.
5. God is 1, Allah is 1 (but Mohammed is the referee).
6. God is first, last and always; the Jews are always caught in the middle.

The Longest-living Jews on Record

Methuselah lived to be 969, as we all know, but no one is quite sure whether the way they measured years in the Bible is the same as we do today. But there *have* been some Jews who have reached goodly ages in modern history, strange as that may seem.

Yaacov Zelovitch of Smolensk, Russia, lived from 1826 until 1932—to the age of 106. When asked the secret of his long life, Mr. Zelovitch replied: "Divorcing my third wife, Bassya. She was driving me crazy with her nagging all the time. If I hadn't got rid of Bassya, I'd have died long ago."

Melvin Zarkai of Beersheva, Israel, lived for 109 years from 1844 until 1953. Mr. Zarkai eagerly told the secret of his longevity: "Moving to the Holy Land in the 1920s was my wisest move. Although it hurt me to leave Newark, New Jersey, it has given me strength not to be hit by United Jewish Appeal solicitors every other week. I've buried dozens of cousins and nephews who were driven into early graves by the ceaseless badgering from the UJA. Here in Israel, they wouldn't *dare* to ask me to give. Hell, I'm on the front line here, you know."

Rivkala Morrison Zelovitch of Smolensk, Russia, lived from 1829 to 1932, for a total of 103 years. When asked her secret of long life, Mrs. Zelovitch replied, "Divorcing my second husband, Yaacov. He was killing me with his complaints, his protests, his *schlemazeldicke* life. If I hadn't divorced Yaacov, I'm sure I never would have made 60, much less 100."

Jewish Origins of Famous Places

Great Britain was named by Shoshana Neuwirth of Johannesburg, South Africa. Previously called Britain, its name was changed after Ms. Neuwirth was asked by the *rebbetzin* of her synagogue: "Nu, so how was Britain?" to which she replied, "Great."

Warsaw, Poland, was given its name by Moishe Warshavsky, who founded it in 803 of the Common Era.

Greenland was named after Chaim Green of Frampol, Poland, who was shipwrecked there trying to escape from his beloved homeland. "The people who someday will have to *stay* on that God-forsaken island should thank their lucky stars that my name isn't the same as my grandfather's—Grenovski," Mr. Green said later, from Sheffield, England.

Glossary

After consulting countless philologists, etymologists, entomologists, semanticists and anti-semanticists, we decided that we'd have to do this glossary ourselves.

The origins of some of the following phrases and words are shrouded in centuries of misty confusion. As you can see below, we are following a great and long tradition.

Abi gezunt (Yiddish): lit., "You should only be healthy." Originally "Abbey Gezunt," a health resort in Lithuania in the Middle Ages.

"Adon Olam" (Middle High Hebrew): lit., "The Last Chance." Composed in the Middle Ages by Menachem ben Menachem Nachum, extolling God's wonders and criticizing Him for making the prayers too long.

Afikoman (Ancient Greek, *A-fi-ko-man*; Modern Greek, *A-fi-ko-person)*: lit., "dessert." To the ancient Greeks, this meant ice cream and slave girls; to today's Jews, a piece of matzah and much-needed prunes.

Aliyah (Hebrew): lit., "to go up." In synagogue, the honour of being called to the Torah; in Zionist parlance, a move to Israel without passing Go and without collecting 200 shekels.

Bar/Bat Mitzvah (upper class Hebrew): lit., "being responsible to perform mitzvahs." Real meaning—skis, stereos, Israeli bonds, alligator shirts, cheques, etc.

Bikur cholim (Hebrew): lit., "visiting the sick." This usually refers to hospital visits. But Moses lived to 120 and Abraham 175 when there were no hospitals. There is a moral here somewhere.

Bima (Japanese, if transistorized): lit., "platform." Where the Torah is read in synagogue; in Japan, where the Tora Tora Tora is read.

"Birkat Hamazon" (Hebrew): lit., "Blessing over Food." More-assimilated Jews call it "Grace after Meals." Far-more-assimilated Jews don't say it at all.

Blintzes (from Russian, *blin*—beat; *Tz*—the Jews): Rallying cry of Cossacks during pogroms of 1900–1906.

Bris (very ancient, painful Hebrew): lit., "covenant." In reality, a minor operation on an eight-day-old Jew of the male persuasion who has no say in the matter.

Bubbe (Hollywood): Friend, buddy, grandmother. If yelled loudly and passionately enough, the word magically brings forward piles of food.

Challah (ancient, stale Hebrew): A big fluffy dog, as in *Lassie Come Home*.

Chazzanim: Enemies of rabbis who consider themselves Pavarottis but are more often Harpo Marxes.

Chometz: lit., "leavened bread." First discovered by Rabbi Moshe Levin; first baked by Rebbetzin Malka Levin.

Fleishig (Yiddish): Fleishig.

Gefilte fish: lit., "stuffed fish," made from pike, carp, white fish, anything semi-fresh and semi-cheap; lacks taste without horseradish.

Gevalt (Yiddish): See *Oy vey iz mir*.

Hazzanim: See Chazzanim. Better yet, don't see or *hear* chazzanim (hazzanim).

Keppel (Yiddish): lit., "head." Usually filled with advanced physics formulae, legal studies, and medical breakthroughs, occasionally topped by *yarmulka*.

Kiddish: An after-*shul nosh* following a *simcha*, paid for by *eltern* or the *bubbe* or *zayde. Farshtay?*

"Kol Nidre": Holy prayer on Yom Kippur evening, meant to fill Jews with fear and trembling for souls, but the boring sermon and Israeli Bond appeal usually do it better.

Kvell (Yiddish): What grandparents do when they hear of grandchildren clerking for Supreme Court justices.

Latke (Hebrew, from ancient Babylonian recipe): *Lat*—much; *Ke*—indigestion.

Lox: Founding partner of firm Lox, Stock and Beryl.

Mazel (Hebrew): lit., "luck." That which any Jew who has made it this far into the twentieth century had lots of.

Mazel tov: lit., "congratulations," as on your new home, new marriage, passing an exam, passing a kidney stone, passing a border checkpoint.

Mensch: lit., "a man," as in "What a mensch!" Not to be confused with *macho*, a term used by Spanish-Portuguese Jews.

Mezuzah: A selection from the Torah placed in a small casing and attached to the doorpost of a Jew's home; lit., "Watch your step!"

Mikvah: Ritual bath, meant to guard life of Jew, even though life guard is usually unnecessary.

Minyan: Quorum of ten men needed for public Jewish prayer, so the nine who can't read Hebrew aren't too embarrassed.

Mishpacha: Everyone who shows up for Passover meal.

Mitzvot (*Mitz*—you better do it; *Vot*—or else): God's divine commandments to His Chosen People, including Helping the Poor, Discovering a Vaccine for Polio, Keeping the Sabbath Day, Overfeeding Children.

Mohel: Ritual circumcizer. Mack the Knife. The Yankee Clipper.

Momzer (Hebrew/Yiddish/Esperanto): The president of your synagogue; your boss; your cousin Simon; your stock broker.

Nachas (after the town in Mississippi): What one feels after joining the $1 Million Insurance Club or selling the most girdles.

Narishkeit (Yiddish): lit., "dumbness"; "stupidity." Dropping out of law school in the last week to pursue Truth; dropping out of medical school at any time to pursue a woman.

Oy vey iz mir. See *Gevalt*.

Payos (Hebrew/Yiddish): lit., "Sideburns run wild."

Pesach: Passover. A time of rejoicing, matzah-consumption, and massive weight-gain.

Pulkas: Thighs. Usually *zoftig*, whether on chicken or turkey. See *zoftig*.

Rebbetzin: Rabbi's wife, as in "Friday, the Rebbetzin Slept Late."

Shacharit: Morning prayers. See *Oy vey iz mir*.

Shaytel: lit., "platinum blonde," or "shocking redhead." A wig worn for modesty. We can't figure it out either.

Shiksa: lit., "beautiful, gorgeous, gracious, attractive, stunning, irresistible." Non-Jewish woman.

Shiva: Seven days of mourning set aside to consider the meaning of life and life insurance.

Shtreimel: Large, furry hat worn by Hassidim, resembling a fox curled up on a bearded Jew's head.

Sukkah: A fragile booth built for holiday of Sukkot. See *Sukkot*.

Sukkot: Holiday during which Jews live in fragile booths. (We hope you have it straight, now).

Tallis: A prayer shawl. Look it up in a good glossary.

Tefillin: Phylacteries. Look it up in a good picture book.

Trefe: Crab. Lobster. Chitlins. Hog jowls. Scallops. Eating at Uncle Kevin's and Auntie Grace's.

Yahrtzeit: Anniversary of someone's death when Jews sit around and discuss how he worked himself into an early grave.

Yarmulka (Yiddish): *Kipah* (Hebrew). *Beanie* (Anti-Semitic). Cap worn 1) as a sign of reverence; 2) to cover bald spot; 3) to protect against sun stroke.

Yerida (Hebrew): lit., "to go down." A term referring to Israelis who leave Promised Land to seek fortune in Golden Land.

Yeshiva Bochers: lit., "students in academies of higher Jewish learning." What's wrong with Harvard or Yale?

Zoftig (Yiddish): lit., *shtark*. *You* know, like your Aunt Yetta's *pulkas*.

Edited by José Druker
Designed by David Shaw
Composed by Attic Typesetting Inc.
Manufactured in the United States of
America by Publishers Press